DEFINITIONS

GIORGIO LOCCHI

DEFINITIONS

THE TEXTS THAT REVOLUTIONIZED NONCONFORMIST CULTURE

ARKTOS
LONDON 2024

ARKTOS
🌐 Arktos.com f fb.com/Arktos ◎ @arktosmedia ✕ arktosjournal

Copyright © 2024 by Arktos Media Ltd.

All rights reserved. No part of this book may be reproduced or utilised in any form or by any means (whether electronic or mechanical), including photocopying, recording or by any information storage and retrieval system, without permission in writing from the publisher.

ISBN
978-1-917646-04-8 (Paperback)
978-1-917646-05-5 (Hardback)
978-1-917646-06-2 (Ebook)

Translation
F. C.

Editing
Constantin von Hoffmeister

Layout
Tor Westman

CONTENTS

Preface: Giorgio Locchi, Theorist of Superhumanism vii

I. DESTINY

Ethology and the Human Sciences 1
History and Destiny 15
Kingdom, Empire, *Imperium* 29
Myth and Community 43

II. ROOTS

Indo-European Identity and the Modern World 53
The Indo-European Cosmogonic Myth: Reconstruction and Relevance 67
Lévi-Strauss and Structural Anthropology 83
Introduction to *The Ring of the Nibelung* 111

III. FIGURES

Nietzsche and His 'Rehabilitators' 137
Regarding *Man and Technics* 149
Armin Mohler and the Conservative Revolution 161
Epilogue: Europe Is Not an Inheritance but a Future Mission 175

L'Institut Iliade for Long European Memory 179

PREFACE

Giorgio Locchi, Theorist of Superhumanism

by Antoine Dresse

T HE NAME Giorgio Locchi has long intrigued me. Some years ago, as I was discovering the works of the so-called 'New Right,' his name appeared here and there in a citation or notes at the bottom of a page and, without being quite sure, I felt I was encountering a man of great intellectual stature. When I read that Guillaume Faye considered him his main inspiration, alongside Nietzsche,[1] my curiosity deepened. However, I was stricken by an initial paradox: in the very country in which he was most involved in the development of an original and profound line of thought, it was almost impossible to find his works. For many years, my understanding of Locchian thinking was therefore limited to certain of his articles published in the journal *Nouvelle École* or to a few concepts, as stimulating as they were mysterious, such as *Superhumanism*, the *Interregnum* or even the spherical conception of time.

My intuitions were confirmed when, at last, thanks to the efforts of his son Pierluigi Locchi, I discovered *Wagner, Nietzsche et le mythe surhumaniste* and the texts you will discover in the present publication. A work to be judged not by its quantity but by the depth of its

---

1   Guillaume Faye, 'Réflexions archéofuturistes inspirée par la pensée de Giorgio Locchi.'

teaching and of the perspectives it unveils. For that is exactly what it is: an *unveiling*. Giorgio Locchi is not only a talented commentator, a pedagogue or a populariser who disinterestedly explains the thought of a Nietzsche or a Heidegger: he is rather 'an awakener and a dynamiter,' as Faye said; a mentor who lets us see the dynamics at work behind two millennia of the history of the West and the forces that are clashing therein. With an audacity that few readers will have the courage to follow, Giorgio Locchi crossed the intellectual Rubicon that is the radical and uncompromising critique of egalitarianism and its corollary, which is nihilism.

Egalitarianism, as Locchi clearly shows, is not only a political programme, merely a social demand pushed to the extreme, nor a somewhat naïve utopia. Egalitarianism is the philosophical expression of an unidimensional and unidirectional conception of history: of history understood as an arrow flying from one point to another, with the whole series of events set between these two points. The mythic formulation of this conception of history is that of Fall and Redemption: of the Fall that plunges mankind into history and of the Redemption that liberates it from history. This morphology of history, which Locchi calls 'segmental,' has fundamentally structured the Western worldview for the last two millennia. The idea that governs it is that man's true being, his essence, is exterior to history; history is merely an accident with respect to the essence of mankind, a passing phase that will be resolved sooner or later. The notion of an 'end of history' may seem to some the symbol *par excellence* of modernity; but it is ultimately nothing other than the logical culmination of an ancient train of thought that has governed and shaped our civilization. Beginning with the Christian myth,[2] egalitarian thinking was first developed concurrently

---

2   Not to be understood as something negative. As Giorgio Locchi himself wrote: 'We call any discourse a "myth" which, as it develops, creates its own language, giving words *new meanings* and appealing through symbols to the imaginations of its audience.' [For this and subsequent citations from Locchi, see 'History and Destiny' below — Tr.].

into more or less sophisticated and utopian ideologies, and then into a conceptual and precise line of thought expressed in a purportedly '*scientific*'[3] form. As Giorgio Locchi wrote:

> We might say, then, that egalitarian *myth*, *ideologies* and purported *science* express progressive levels of consciousness of a single will. Products of one and the same *mentality*, they all present the same basic structure. Naturally, the same goes for the conceptions of history they generate, which only differ in form and the languages they discursively deploy. Whatever its form, the egalitarian vision of history is *eschatological*, assigning history a negative value, and only assigning it a meaning inasmuch as historical movement tends towards its own negation and end.

Thus, human history, vale of tears or battlefield of the class-struggle, is an unbearable story of oppression and alienation. And as such, if man is to recover his authentic dignity, it must come to an end.

But if Giorgio Locchi has proven, remarkably, the unity of the egalitarian schema that has structured our consciousness these last two millennia, he has also and especially unveiled the *rupture* that began to open around a century and a half ago. This rupture, which is radically opposed to the schema of thought that establishes and undergirds the theologies, philosophies, ideologies and political structures of the West, he named the *Superhumanist tendency*. This tendency, inaugurated, in his view, by Wagner and Nietzsche, was first formulated theoretically by Locchi, allowing us correctly to clarify and distinguish two irremediably antagonistic conceptions of history.

If the egalitarian conception of history is segmental, lodged between an *alpha* and an *omega*, the Superhumanist conception of history is 'open' and distinguished by the 'innocence of becoming,' as Nietzsche put it. This new vision of history is founded upon a new intuition of man, history and the world. This is the intuition of the

---

[3] Marxism is obviously the most striking form example of the transformation of the egalitarian myth into (pseudo)science; but it should not be taken for the only example in existence. Contemporary leftist thinking claims to be just as scientific with its 'postcolonial studies' and 'gender studies.'

tridimensional character of man's temporality, of the 'historicality' of *Dasein* (Heidegger).[4] Against the unidimensional and linear conception of time, Wagner, Nietzsche and, in turn, conservative-revolutionary writers set a tridimensional conception of historical temporality, expressed less theoretically or conceptually than imagistically. Time is no longer conceived as an arrow but a 'Sphere.' The use of a guiding image, a '*Leitbild*,' was indispensable for overthrowing a language moulded and impregnated for centuries, even in its rationality, by the unidimensional conception of time. Heidegger's great merit, in the first part of his work, is precisely to deconstruct this received language and to conceptualize, on the basis of a new language, the tridimensional character of historico-existential temporality in which past, present and future coexist at every moment, forming the three dimensions of *every historical moment*.

Such an intuition will seem rather complex on first sight; but this complexity comes from our habituation to thinking of time as a mere succession of events, each following another without mutual relation or influence. Now, what Nietzsche showed was that the past need not be seen as something fixed forever, which *was* once and for all and which the present leaves behind. A historical event, as such, is never *finished*. From a strictly linear perspective on history, such facts as the fall of Rome, the birth of the Protestant Reformation o the Second World War are entirely dead. But they are only so from a strictly spatiotemporal perspective: for their *meaning* is by no means dead. The meaning of a historical event is always latently subsistent and retains the power to manifest to its full extent. Similarly, the future is no longer the necessary effect of all the causes that precede and determine it in time. The future of an action, once taken, is to be found equally in its consequences and in our decisions which shape the future in the present.

---

4 See, inter alia, *Being and Time*, part 1, div. 2, v. — Tr.

At history's every moment, at every 'actuality,' past and future are, so to speak, *called into question*, formed by a new perspective, forming a *new truth*. Taking another image, we might say that the past is simply the project to which man conforms his historical action, a project he seeks to realize in accordance with an image he makes himself, which he strives to incarnate. So the past reappears as a *prefiguration of the future*. It is, in the true sense of the word, the future's 'imagination.' This is one meaning of the mytheme of the Eternal Return.

The consequence of such an intuition of time is unavoidable: history is open; man himself makes it. Man's true being is no longer outside a history which acts upon him (through Grace or through economic and material forces) but, on the contrary, in his very historicity. Thus, his freedom of becoming is forcefully asserted — but with the real possibility of deciding between the *end of history* and its *regeneration*.

'Man is a rope strung between beast and Superman,' said Nietzsche;[5] and it is precisely between these two conceptions of history, between the *last man* of the end of history and the *Superman* of its regeneration, that this rope is to be found. The linear or the spherical conception of history; egalitarianism or Superhumanism: these are the two great tendencies of our age, says Giorgio Locchi: a choice that heralds a radical revolution conceived as a renovation of origins. Whence the publication of the present work.

If the essay dedicated to *Wagner, Nietzsche and the Superhumanist Myth* contains the author's most essential insights into the Superhumanist tendency and the spherical conception of history, then the dozen texts that make up *Definitions* are crucial for unveiling the Lochian teaching in all its depth. Wherefore are gathered in one volume almost all Giorgio Locchi's contributions to the journal *Nouvelle École*, which represent the heart of his teaching to the 'New Right.' This book's various essays are skeleton-keys to the various questions that animated Locchi's thinking. If it is generally thought that his main contribution was to the philosophy of history, the reader will discover

---

5 *Thus Spake Zarathustra*, 'Zarathustra's Prologue,' 4. — Tr.

in these documents numerous paths of extraordinarily fertile reflection which will philosophically support the renovative rupture that the 'Superhumanist principle' has made in the history of thinking.

This anthology offers, then, the double advantage of a complete and detailed introduction to Giorgio Locchi's philosophical questioning and a handy complement to the reading of the author's other works. Indeed, here one will find many common themes, more synthetically developed and more easily accessible, alongside new themes developed only on these essays.

Giorgio Locchi's thinking, then, lies in the wake of the works of Wagner, Nietzsche, the conservative revolution in Germany and Heidegger,[6] of which it is a *critical* and *creative* rereading. This Superhumanist adventure, says Locchi, begins in the artistic works of Richard Wagner, who claimed to make a new 'beginning' and to lead mankind to his *regeneration*. It is for this reason that we ought to see the *Ring* or *Parsifal* as the representation of a new and founding myth by which a new historical tendency emerges and takes shape. Nietzsche then followed and deepened this tendency both critically, exposing the relativity of the absolute principles proclaimed by egalitarianism, and poetically (from the Greek verb ποιεῖν, to create), striving to give birth to a new type of man, attached to new values and acting upon the principles of a *Superhumanist* ethic.

But the analysis of this philosophy and music of becoming is made difficult by the fact that their language is one of myth, which, by definition, makes it difficult to express in rational and conceptual language. Giorgio Locchi's major contribution, then, is in this revelation, in the *un*-veiling of this myth, thereby allowing its meaning to be deployed to its full extent. Indeed, it is difficult to remain unscathed by a reading of Giorgio Locchi and to return to his precursors' works as if nothing had happened. The depth of his teaching is certainly vertiginous; and the

---

[6] Giorgio Locchi's essay 'Heidegger et la révolution conservatrice [Heidegger and the Conservative Revolution]' has recently been rediscovered and is to be published in future.

radicalism of his thinking precludes — for those who consent to follow it — the least concession to egalitarianism. Naturally, this radicalism also largely explains Locchi's solitude and his exclusion from academic *milieux*, where philosophy is understood as the mere pronouncement of conformist and jargonizing commonplaces. But it may well be that, thirty years after the Roman philosopher's death, his *oeuvre* will at last find the public it deserves in those who do not take it as an act of aggression to be shaken in their certainties.

According to Spengler, the history of the West will very soon reach its end. But as Giorgio Locchi judiciously remarks, it is rather to the end of all history that the West is tending, hoping to find immobile happiness in regression. It is therefore imperative that those who refuse this end of history take up the work undertaken by Giorgio Locchi and pursued by Guillaume Faye with his concept of *Archaeofuturism*, developing their own creative critique of egalitarian thinking. Against those who only find history's meaning in its negation, we set a conception of man who has a future only in the regeneration of historical time.

If the various egalitarian conceptions of history in their eschatological aspects today reach a consensus, in that they all follow a segmental schema aiming at a final point at which Good will reign for eternity, then Giorgio Locchi was one of the first to bring it to light. And he was also the first to take full account of the Nietzschean 'eternal return of the same' and to propose the spherical conception of time in radical opposition. Therefore, it behoves the European intellectual, all those who no longer submit to the great egalitarian dogmas, to take up this reflection where Giorgio Locchi left off and to think new principles, new post-Western and post-egalitarian values equal to the task, and thereby to put an end to a long procession of illusions. The Locchian *oeuvre* is not a perfectly finished thing, of course; and it would be fruitful to pursue his analyses in a search for precursors of the Superhumanist tendency among thinkers like Carlyle or Herder, for example; but it cannot be ignored any longer. Radical and exacting, his thought calls us more than ever to develop a strategy for the *Interregnum*, that period of *anticipation*, destined to conclude either in the triumph of the egalitarian tendency and the 'end of history' or in the 'regeneration of history' and the European assertion of what Locchi names *Superhumanism*. This anticipation may seem rather long and dark, but even after the darkest night the dawn-glow is bound to rise.

I

DESTINY

This essay is the last text Giorgio Locchi published in *Nouvelle École* (no. 33, summer 1979). Here, Locchi examines the relationships between the results of ethology and sociobiology and the propositions of Arnold Gehlen's philosophical anthropology — propositions our author helped to make known in France and Italy and developed in original directions. Of necessity, he approaches certain ultimate questions regarding the specifically human and the way to approach research in this field, which is still regarded with suspicion on account of blatantly ideological prejudice. The conclusion of this essay in particular is also an initial formulation of the open theory of history which is introduced in the first chapter of his *Wagner, Nietzsche et le mythe surhumaniste* (Paris: Institut Iliade–La Nouvelle Librairie, coll. Agora, 2022).

1

Ethology and the Human Sciences

A FUNDAMENTAL objection of a gnoseological order has very often been levelled against the human sciences, which aims to deny them the status of genuine sciences. The human sciences have found it impossible to adequately define their object, which is man himself. Since man is both its subject and its object, the necessary distinction between subject and object is in this instance impossible. Therefore, every *scientific* enterprise concerning the human as such is doomed to failure. Clearly this gnoseological objection rests upon a conception of science inherited from the delusive positivism of the nineteenth century and is now outdated. The adventure of microphysics has also demonstrated that, even in physics, the separation of (human) subject and (physical) object is never perfectly achieved — indeed, that it is unachievable on account of the uncertainty principle formulated by Heisenberg.

It is from quite another, more contemporary perspective that the Frankfurt School has joined the war against the human sciences or, to adopt its own terminology, against all 'anthropology.' This school, whose masters were the philosophers and sociologists Theodor Adorno and Max Horkheimer, along with the younger Marcuse, and whose most prominent representative these days is Jürgen Habermas, bases its argument upon an indisputable conception of science. All science gives rise to a *technology* which renders its object available to man. The man of science, rightly understood, may be personally disinterested, motivated by a straightforward will to knowledge. But it is nonetheless true that any definition of an object verified, necessarily, by experiment, gives rise to a practical technique for the determination of this object which can then be manipulated by the *technician* for his own purposes. Anthropology, taking man for its object, yields techniques for the manipulation of man by man — constituting object-men distinct from subject-men.

The Frankfurt School does not seem to mean to deduce the formal *impossibility* of any anthropology. It does not maintain — this, at least, is my impression — that anthropology cannot constitute a genuine *science*. But it pronounces a *moral* condemnation of anthropology as an 'instrument' for the domination of man by man. Disciples of the Frankfurt School are therefore morally obliged to actively oppose every positive anthropology by means of a corresponding 'negative' anthropology. That is what is called *critical theory*. Against every positive assertion concerning man is levelled a radical critique; against every technology bearing upon man, an 'emancipatory' counter-technology.

Though it grew out of Marxism and aimed, from the beginning, to develop a Marxist sociology, the Frankfurt School has ended up detaching itself from Marxism. More precisely, while it remains faithful to the ethic of egalitarian communism, it denounces the *optimist* illusions of Classical Marxism, asserting that Marxism's ultimate goal, the advent of the 'Reign of Liberty' and the total emancipation of man, never can be attained, but that it might nevertheless be possible to approach it ever more closely, asymptotically, so long as negative anthropology remains practically vigilant against every form of positive anthropology that history might throw up. This is an ideological, quasi-religious position which clearly continues, in a modern context, the eternal biblical 'No' to every Faustian enterprise, to every attempt to become 'like unto God.' Moreover, Horkheimer, the leader of the school, expressly refers to the God of the Bible, the perfect and exemplary image of being, indescribable by definition. Negative anthropology is thus the continuation of apophatic religion *par excellence*.

It seems necessary to me to recall the traditional gnoseological objection to the human sciences, alongside the Frankfurt School's moral condemnation of all positive anthropology, for purposes of clarification. Any discussion of the human sciences must be rather complex; and I should first like to specify my own position. The gnoseological objection to the human sciences seems to me utterly without foundation. I recognize the possibility of the human sciences' reaching the status of genuine *science*. Moreover, my ideological positions are totally opposed to those of the Frankfurt School. These preliminaries ought to avoid any confusion. I am therefore more at ease to express my distrust towards the human sciences as presently practised and to say that, in my view, in the present state of affairs, *there are still no genuine human sciences*. The chemistry of man is yet to come. In this domain, we are still doing alchemy.

The Four Levels of the Real

The culprit is what is called the *reductionist* tendency in the human sciences. Explicitly or otherwise, it is near-universally thought possible to reduce man to pure *naturality*, that is, to pure biology, or even, as Mr. Lévi-Strauss once seriously suggested, to physicochemistry. It is even said that man is a 'recent invention,' his existence a deceptive illusion. One can surely see the marks of an ideological prejudice in this attitude, the reflection of the will to self-destruction of a civilization in crisis, compulsively questioning the *idea* of man around which it has always revolved, determined to halt the emergence of any new 'human idea of man.' But it is also true that we live in a period of transition — that the recent domestication of energy has revealed levels of the real whose existence we had scarcely suspected, and that it is very difficult to distinguish one level from the next. The world of *matter* splits into two: a microphysical world, the world of the elementary, whose laws are very different, has suddenly emerged alongside the macrophysical world. Moreover, the phenomenon of *life*, till now muddled with the material under the general heading, 'Nature,' is beginning to assert its independence from the physicochemical, while the *historicity* of man appears in its fulness, making a fourth level of the real. These four levels (macrophysical, microphysical, biological, human) are themselves established as the peculiar objects of four different branches of science. But an archaic cast of mind refuses to admit this evidence and, alas, even taints certain men of science. And so Einstein, author of the theory of relativity, obstinately refused to admit the principle of indeterminacy, saying, 'God does not play dice...'

The hermeneutic dispute provoked by the theory of quanta clearly shows the difficulty of definition one level of the real in relation to another. But it has also indicated, thanks to the Göttingen School, what might be the solution to the problem. The macrophysical and microphysical levels obey *different but non-contradictory laws*. From the practical point of view, that is, the human, the laws of one serve as the limit-case of the other. Everything is a matter of limits. Thus, the biological law of life does not 'contradict' any physicochemical law. It is fitted uniquely to the living, governing a domain of no concern (as limit-case) to physicochemical laws. Similarly, what pertains to man does not 'contradict' biological laws — of which man constitutes the *unique* limit-case — but simply *overcomes* them. And that aspect of the human which overcomes the biological to constitute a fourth level of the real is what is conventionally called the *historical* level.

As I will come to say, once one frees oneself from the old mentality, one is able to construct the definitions that follow from the four levels of the real, abandoning the temptation to *reduce* one to the other (in whatever sense). In the context of this exposition, I will stick to the distinction between the *biological* and the *historical*.

The great merit of biological anthropology and comparative ethology is to have clearly shown man's irreducibility to the biological. I must add, though, that bioanthropologists and ethologists often fail to draw all the conclusions that follow from this point. The best definition of the living being is derived from the discoveries of molecular biology and ethology. The characteristic of the living is, on the one hand, to tend to reproduce itself identically and, on the other, to be directly bound to a *specific environment* created *ipso facto* by its sensory apparatus. This intimate relationship between a species and its specific environment constitutes the biological phenomenon called *instinct*. An animal's specific environment can be more or less expansive, but it always has some limit. An animal has an innate awareness of this specific environment — and of nothing else. The elements of his specific milieu have precise meanings for an animal, constituting unequivocal *signals* to which he responds with *determined* behaviours. This discovery, the credit for which is due to Jakob von Uexküll, is fundamental: for it clearly shows how man represents a *limit-case* of the living and thereby overcomes it. We might say that *man has no specific environment*, or, to say the same thing in different words, that *he can adapt himself to any environment*. Having no direct bond to a specific environment, *he has no instincts*, or, to say the same thing in different words, *he has every instinct*. Arnold Gehlen admirably encapsulated this state of affairs in his formula *Weltoffenheit*, that 'openness to the world' characteristic of man. 'Specific environment' in German is *Art-Umwelt*. An animal is not aware that his reality, the only with existence and meaning for him, is nothing more than a segment defined by his sensory apparatus. Man's sensory apparatus is open to virtually *all reality*, to the whole world; but the elements of this world he perceives never have a precise, *univocal* meaning for him. In other words, the signals he receives never strictly determine him. Rather, they represent 'enigmas' for him to decipher, requiring him to *decide* between different possible behaviours. An animal knows everything, directly, about his specific environment. His behaviour — like his 'knowledge' — is strictly *programmed*. Man, having no specific environment, *knows nothing in advance*. He must therefore *understand, experiment, assign meaning*, always making *precise decisions* between diverse possibilities.

At this point, we ought to agree upon the meaning of some terms. Like any living being, man has organic urges. Like any living being, he is subject to external pressures — and, clearly, as much as any animal, has only his own body directly available to him. For reasons far from scientific, some have tried to deny that man is *naturally* subject to certain urges, the urge to aggression, for example. Writers such as Robert Ardrey and Konrad Lorenz have tried to deflate these denials and have demonstrated their absurdity. Moreover, ethologists like Irenäus Eibl-Eibesfeldt have cut those sociologists who claim that man is naturally and exclusively determined by aggressive urges down to size. In reality, man is constantly assailed by the most richly contradictory urges. Except, in his case, these urges *never have a precise object*. They remain, so to speak, 'blind.' It is in this sense that we may say that man 'has no instincts' — and that the *purpose* of his behaviour is always up to him to determine. Unlike the animal, who responds to every urge, whether endogenous or triggered by signals from his specific environment, with behaviour aimed at a precise goal, an object determined in advance, man is given neither a 'natural' nor an 'automatic' response. He must reflet and *decide* between many equally possible responses. Man must *programme himself*. This is not a matter of mere training, as we see among the higher animals, which is naturally predetermined by a 'genetic fingerprint.' Man can always decide between multiple self-programmes, and even between programmes of opposite tendencies. We are all familiar with these programmes: they are called 'cultures.' The very multiplicity of cultures within the human species clearly attests to decisions freely made. There are *multiple* human cultures but only *one* human nature.

To fully understand the human phenomenon, which is both *culture in space* and, as we shall see, *history in time*, we must get past any equivocality stemming from a terminology bound to a defunct vision of reality. Ethologists sometimes say that man is naturally endowed with determined, innate behavioural mechanisms favourable to the preservation of the species. Prof. Eibl-Eibesfeldt, for example, has said as much. I agree, so long as we do not muddle *behavioural mechanisms* with *behaviour tout court* — saying, for example, that man makes use of a specifically human body, possessing certain faculties and potentialities innately. Eibl-Eibesfeldt (who uses the term 'programmed man,' mistakenly, in my view) writes:

> Pre-programmed man is our problem; but he is also our hope. Our problem because a great part of what is innate in us is not adapted to modern society. On the other hand, we find in these assets a common heritage. Men are separated into cultures as if these constitute distinct species; but at the biological level, men form a unity. They share certain universal behaviours as well as certain moral norms.[1]

Let me be frank and admit that this discourse leaves me perplexed. We are told that, from the biological perspective, men constitute a unity, that is, a species — which is quite obvious. We are also told that they are 'separated into cultures as if these constitute distinct species' — which is also quite obvious. But what does this mean if we are committed to define the human scientifically in relation to the biological? The answer seems to me to be that *the biological unity of the species does not constrain man*; that *man himself decides and defines what belongs to his species and what does not belong*. What is innate in man pertains to his *natural* species, with all that that entails. But, again, this does not determine him, since he remains free to define the objects of his species' behaviour and his interspecific behaviour. You can speak of a 'universal moral norm' if you like; but concretely, this norm relies upon man's amical relations as *culturally* and not biologically determined objects. And while some see an opportunity to return to the biological unity of the species, the better to adapt to life in modern society, I will limit myself — without even asking whether this adaptation might be rather be found in the opposite direction — to the obvious: to wit, that to reduce man to a biological species is to *strip him of his humanity, of his historicity*. This, of course, is the unconscious desire of societies exhausted by history. It might even be an achievable goal. Let me repeat, for clarity's sake, that it is not my desire.

---

1   *Der vorprogrammierte Mensch* (Munich: Deutscher Taschenbuch Verlag, 1973), p. 13. — Tr.

But let us return to the historical problem, that is, to the *creation of man by man* and to the *creation of cultures*. We stated above that man is free to decide, that nature imposes nothing upon him, nothing contrary to the *purposes* of his behaviour. This means, on the other hand, that man is *obliged to set the purposes of his behaviour*, a vital obligation amounting to his determination of himself *as man*. The Ancients were well aware of this negative determination and the authentic freedom that it guarantees. They speak of it in their myths. Negative determination was known to them as *fatum*, 'destiny', which does not contradict man but confronts him with a decision. Like Hercules at the fork in the path, man can always opt out of his heroic destiny for something more 'humble', for a return to 'nature'. But the mark of the hero, of man *par excellence*, is to choose—with Hercules, Achilles or Ulysses—the exhilarating adventure of a life, however *fatal*, that would be 'like unto the gods'.

Freedom, in this sense, is of course relative. But it is in precisely this respect that it is an authentic freedom. There is none but relative freedom. Let us expand on this point. The problem of freedom has always been one of the highest points of philosophical reflection, a question arising from Reason's notorious aporias, that is, from two entirely antithetical and mutually exclusive answers. This is down to our always having asked the question of freedom in the metaphysically absolute; and in the absolute, freedom shades into its opposite, predetermination. In reality, man can only be relatively free, since he is always compelled to decide between diverse, even opposite, options, *free to decide but compelled, and compelling himself, to decide*. Therefore, biological law, as the law of the species, determines man negatively—while it determines an animal positively—*leaving him solely responsible for himself*. This freedom is authentic because man remains free to abolish his own freedom in the ultimate decision. Man can even renounce life, consciously, by suicide, if it seems to him to be the only means of realizing the idea he has formed of man. Moreover, this is true not only of individuals but of societies. Think, for example, of the Amazonian tribes who let themselves die out rather than conform to a Western civilizational model.

Man's *exercise* of this authentic freedom is *history itself*. History reproduces man's original condition before life, the necessity to *freely decide*, at every moment and for every human being in an ever-renewed form. Man must create himself every moment, invent himself every moment: for at every moment the human equation remains the same. Then arises the problem of the ambiguity of every culture with its own idea of man. We might say that *culture is the nature of man*. This is true in two senses. Lacking a natural programme with fixed objects and goals, man must give himself a cultural programme, a *culture*. Through the creation of this culture, he *becomes man*; he *creates himself*. But once created, the nature of this culture — artificial, if you insist, but nature nonetheless — is established. It thereby becomes a compulsory law governing men from generation to generation, just as the biological law of the species governs the animal. For man's historical condition to be preserved, culture, like nature, must only determine man *negatively*, both *imposing decision* upon him and *leaving him free in this decision*. Ultimately, an individual may decide against the culture in which he finds himself.

Cultural Model and Social Type

This helps us understand the movement of history and allows us, or so it seems to me, to explain the duration, slow transformation, rise, decline and death of cultures. Man is a social animal, even if his social determination is negative. Which is to say that man, to realize himself, must both create himself and *create his own society*. Now, as regards self-creation, human individuals manifest and realize different values. There are, as every man knows — even if it displease him — two *limit-degrees* of man's historical value: what we call *mass-man* and, at the other extreme, the *founding hero*. The first is 'non-humanized man,' whose urges are not yet culturally determined. Incapable of determining himself, he is momentarily, erratically determined from without my chance or compulsion, and above all by human compulsion. He follows without knowing he follows. Contrarily, the second is a man with an *original* idea of himself and his society which he *realizes* — thereby creating *cultural fact* (or new cultural fact). These, as we said, are the limit-degrees of man's value. In the relativity of the real, practically every individual shares in both the 'mass' and the 'creative' to variable degrees, of course. It is precisely this that allows for social organization and for the social game that plays out between antagonistic poles within one culture.

A culture's pre-existence is a boon for the man in whom the mass-value predominates. By means of social traditions and education, he can be made to repeat the process of human self-creation offered by the cultural *model*, that is, to represent the *social type*. He is thereby fully integrated into the social group, the *people*. The simplest form of the repetition of this process of integration, codified in each culture, is the initiatory rite. In modern society, this process has been muddled with the educational system, which is reinforced with all-too-familiar techniques of conditioning.

One might think that, contrarily, an individual in whom the creative value predominates would be led to reject the culture he inherits, and its values, in order to assert his own originality. But this is only true of very elderly cultures, maladapted to historical exigencies. In a young culture, whose 'type' preserves its humanizing force, the creator takes charge of *both the preservation and the perfection of the social type*. He strives to teach it through his example, and thereby asserts himself as a personality. Moreover, in a young culture, the cultural model remains relatively open and always appears as a project in the process of realization. It is therefore always felt to be open to *new interpretations*; and this lasts as long as there are domains of man's activity in which this model has not yet been incarnated. The *creative* value is the historical value *par excellence*. This is why we have always venerated founding heroes, geniuses, great artists. This is why we value the original more highly than the copy, even if the latter conforms to the former in every respect. But 'personality,' let us emphasize, is not the exaltation of individual egoism. Rather, it is a society's highest expression, its highest conscience, so to speak, and its superior will. 'Personality' strives restlessly to incarnate its highest idea of itself *and of its other*, that is, its own society. 'Personality' proves itself by responding to the sociocultural imperative of a given historical moment. It is recognized, accepted and followed because, in so doing, it satisfies the unconscious aspirations of a community or people. There is always something sacrificial in 'personality'; and this sacrifice might extend to the ultimate renunciation. This is why we have always hero-worshipped whoever extinguishes himself for the good of his society or culture. Taking charge of a society, the hero occupies the pinnacle of the social hierarchy *by right*.

When a culture has had its hour in the sun and no longer responds to human needs, the mass no longer receives a valid 'type' with which to identify and through which to gain an authentically human stature. It is plunged into the miseries of the state of indeterminate nature. Then comes what is judiciously called the *advent of the masses* — chaotic 'massification.' Then, too, a hero may arise who, growing aware of his society's and his culture's decomposition, sets in motion the necessary *revolution* — an act of *conservation* of man's mortally endangered historical condition.

Our culture and our societies have been decomposing for some time. The crisis endlessly worsens. The rise of the human sciences themselves is one of the most glaring manifestations of this crisis; and still more is the inability of these sciences to push beyond the search for a new definition of man, for a new 'idea of man.' The pluralism and contradictoriness of the definitions proposed (though all inspired by one and the same egalitarian ideology) clearly shows the disaggregation of our societies, the degradation of extant cultures. And these disciplines' conscious or unconscious but invariable fall into biological, even physiochemical *reductionism* makes palpable the magnitude of the danger that threatens us. For this reductionism is the most obvious expression, not only of society's disbelief in man's capacity to take charge of himself, but also of a sort of will to self-destruction stimulated by the dream of a permanent return to the beatific state of the species, cradled by a nature willing to take charge of man as it takes charge of any other species.

From a gnoseological perspective, there is something paradoxical in reductionist human science, in that it negates the specificity of its own object and, in so doing, strips itself of its status as a distinct science, to become a sort of branch of zoology or chemistry. In terms of scientific value, all reductionist theories must be considered false. Biology and comparative ethology have proven the impossibility of reducing man to pure biology, even while certain biologists and ethologists refuse, given the climate of their times, to follow the logical consequences of their discoveries. An authentically human science must be based upon a human *definition of man that recognizes historicity as characteristic of human reality*. Consequently, its field of experimentation and verification is to be found nowhere else but in history: *history that has been finished and history that is yet to be made*.

Since man is free, since he becomes and creates himself from generation to generation, the broadest and deepest expression of human science can only define the *decisions* offered to mankind. And this means that its 'predictions' must always come in the form of alternatives between two limit-ideas of man to come. Of course, the applied human sciences can always yield techniques for the 'manipulation of man by man,' but always the manipulation of the mass or type by a 'personality' rooted in a specific culture. Historical science, as such, must take man in his totality as its object: man in his historicity and his constitutive ambiguity arising from the opposition of one 'personality' against another, and of one manifest idea of man against another. Were it otherwise, man, let us repeat, would not be free — his future would be predetermined, written in advance by someone other than himself. Nietzsche once said that history is written by giants, calling one another across the silence of centuries.² But those giants might also call the heart of the present across the silence of multitudes. In one case as in the other, the response must always come as an implacable and merciless defiance.

Many think that Giorgio Locchi's most important contribution to twentieth-century philosophy belong to the domain of the philosophy of history. The two central elements of this contribution are, on one side, the identification of mythical, ideological and synthetic (or scientific) phases as the archetypal phases of historical tendencies and, on the other, a complete explication of the 'spherical' vision of history introduced by Wagnerial and Nietzschean superhumanism, which we find adopted explicitly in, for example, Martin Heidegger, Armin Mohler and Alain de Benoist (see *Les idées à l'endroit*, or even *Comment peut-on être païen?*).³ This article, which appeared as 'L'Histoire' ('History') in *Nouvelle École* (nos. 27–8, autumn–winter 1975), represents the initial formulation of the author's 'open theory of history.' It would be translated into Spanish and Italian, among others, before being revised and rewritten directly in German in a much-enlarged version referring to the thought of Martin Heidegger, the French translation of which is in preparation. The theme would be reworked and amplified a third time in the first chapter of *Wagner, Nietzsche et le mythe surhumaniste*, published in this Agora series.

---

2 *Untimely Meditations*, 2, 'On the Use and Abuse of History for Life,' 9. — Tr.
3 The latter translated into English as *How to Be a Pagan* (Atlanta, GA, 2004). — Tr.

2

History and Destiny

THESE DAYS, everyone is wondering about the 'meaning of history,' that is, the *purpose* and *meaning* of historical phenomena. The aim of this article is to examine our epoch's answers to this double question, and to reduce them, despite their apparent variety, to two thoroughly antagonistic and contradictory basic types.

But first we must throw some light on the signification we shall give, from the off, to the word 'history.' Questions of vocabulary are important. We sometimes speak of 'natural history,' the 'history of the cosmos,' 'life-history.' This is surely a matter of analogy. But every analogy, while it highlights a poetic similarity, also implies a logical difference. In reality, the macrophysical universe has no history. As we perceive it, as we represent it, it simply changes its *configuration* over time. Nor does life have a history. Its future is an *evolution*; it evolves.

By history we understand the *way of becoming proper to man as such* (and man alone). Only man *develops historically*. Therefore, to ask the question of the meaning of history, that is, of its goal and signification, is to wonder if man himself, who is in history and who (willingly or not) makes history, has a meaning, and whether his participation in history is a rational attitude or not.

Three Successive Periods

Today, history is condemned from all sides. This is nothing new, of course. But today the condemnation is more vehement, more explicit than ever. We are asked to condemn history definitively, with no chance for appeal. History, we are told, is the consequence of man's alienation. We invoke, propose, project the *end of history*. We preach a return to a sort of enriched state of nature, an end to growth, the resolution of conflict, the return to tranquil and serene equilibrium, to a modest but guaranteed happiness for all living things. The names of a few theorists come to mind here, first of all, Herbert Marcuse and Claude Lévi-Strauss, whose ideas are well known.

The notion of the *end of history* may seem as modern as can be. In fact, it is no such thing. Upon examination, one sees that this notion is simply the logical conclusion of a way of thinking at least two thousand years old, and which has, for the last two thousand years, dominated and *formed* what we now call 'Western civilization.' This is *egalitarian thinking*. It expresses an egalitarian will, at first instinctual and almost blind, but which has, by our own time, become fully conscious of its aspirations and ultimate objective. And this ultimate objective of egalitarian thought is the end of history, the *exit* from history.

Over the centuries, egalitarian thought has moved through three successive periods. In the first, corresponding to the birth and development of Christianity, it took the form of a *myth*. This term, let us be clear, is not meant pejoratively. We call any discourse a 'myth' which, as it develops, creates its own language, giving words *new meanings* and appealing through symbols to the imaginations of its audience. Myth's structural elements are called *mythemes*. These consist in *unities of opposites* which, not yet separated, remain hidden, even invisible.

In the process of historical development, the unity of these mythemes ruptures, giving birth to competing ideologies. So Christianity's mythemes gave birth to competing churches, theologies and, ultimately, ideologies (such as those of the French and American Revolutions). These ideologies' emergence and diffusion corresponds to egalitarianism's second period. Unlike myth, *ideologies* lay down principles for action; but they do not draw out their consequences, making their practice hypocritical, sceptical or naïvely optimistic. We come at last to the third period, in which the contradictory notions engendered by the original mythemes dissolve into the unity of a synthetic concept. Egalitarian thought, now animated by a will grown fully conscious, expresses itself in a purportedly 'scientific' form. It declares itself *science*. This step corresponds to the development of Marxism and its derivatives.

We might say, then, that egalitarian *myth*, *ideologies* and purported *science* express progressive levels of consciousness of a single will. Products of one and the same *mentality*, they all present the same basic structure. Naturally, the same goes for the conceptions of history they generate, which only differ in form and the languages they discursively deploy. Whatever its form, the egalitarian vision of history is *eschatological*, assigning history a negative value, and only assigning it a meaning inasmuch as historical movement tends towards its own negation and end.

Restoration at a Specific Moment

When we examine pagan Antiquity, we see that it oscillated between two visions of history, of which one was simply the relative antithesis of the other. Both conceive historical becoming as a succession of instants in which every present delimits the past, on one hand, and the future on the other. The first vision presents a *cyclical* image of historical becoming. It implies the eternal repetition of instants, phases or particular periods. This is expressed by the formula *Nihil sub sole novi* ('Nothing new under the sun').[1] The second, which went onto assimilate the first, imagines a straight line with a beginning but no end, or at least no imaginable or foreseeable end.

Christianity effected a sort of synthesis of these two ancient visions of history, substituting them with a conception we might call 'linear,' but which is really *segmental*. In this vision, history has a beginning, but also an end. It is simply an episode, an incident in mankind's

---

1   *Ecclesiastes*, 1.9. — Tr.

existence. Man's true being is outside history. And the end of history is supposed to restore him by sublimating him, as it was in the beginning. In this fragmentary vision, we find a *conclusion by restoration at a particular moment*, as in the cyclical vision; but unlike the cycle, this moment takes place outside history, outside historical becoming. It is not so much a matter of restoration as of fixation in a changeless eternity. Historical development is *completed*, goes no further. As in the vision of a straight line of perpetual progression, the segmental vision gives history a beginning, but to this beginning is added an end. Man's eternity is no longer one of *becoming* but one of *being*.

From the Christian perspective, that incidental episode called history is a veritable curse. History results from God's condemnation of man to misfortune, labour, sweat and blood, in payment for an error. Mankind, having lived in happy innocence in the Garden of Eden, is *condemned to history* because Adam, his forefather, broke divine commandment, tasted the fruit of the Tree of Knowledge, and longed to equal God. As an original sin, Adam's error taints every individual who comes into this world. It is inexpiable by definition: for the plaintiff is God himself.

But God in his infinite goodness is willing to undergo the expiation himself. He makes himself man and incarnates in the person of Jesus. The sacrifice of the Son of God situates the vital fact of Redemption within historical becoming. Of course, this only concerns those individuals touched by Grace. But it makes possible the slow advent of the end of history, for which the Communion of Saints must now prepare mankind. At last, a day will come when the forces of Good and Evil meet in battle, leading to the Last Judgement and the establishment of the Kingdom of Heaven, whose dialectical counterpart is the depths of Hell.

Eden prior to the beginning of history; original sin; expulsion from the Garden; crossing the vale of tears we call this world, the scene of historical becoming; *Redemption*; the *Communion of Saints*; *apocalyptic battle* and the *Last Judgement*; the *end of history* and the establishment of the *Kingdom of Heaven*. These are the mythemes that structure Christianity's mythical vision of history, in which mankind's historical becoming is assigned a purely negative value and the meaning of an expiation.

The Marxist Vision

The same mythemes are found, in a secularized and purportedly scientific form, in the Marxist vision of history. (We do not intend our use of the term 'Marxist' as a contribution to the debate, currently very fashionable, over 'what Marx actually thought.' Karl Marx thought very different things throughout his life; and one could spend hours in search of the 'true' Marx. Here, we mean *received* Marxism, which has long meant, and which still, in the last analysis, means the doctrines of the communist parties and states following Lenin's interpretations.) This doctrine presents history as the result of *class-struggle*, that is, a struggle between human groups defined by their economic conditions.

This vision's prehistorical Garden of Eden is the 'primitive communism' practiced by man before he plunged into a purely predatory state of nature. As man in Eden was constrained by God's commandments, so prehistoric communist societies lived under the pressure of poverty. This pressure led to the development of means of agricultural production; but these inventions proved a curse. For they imply not only the exploitation of nature by man but the division of labour, the exploitation of man by man and, consequently, the *alienation* of every man from himself. Class-struggle is the implicit consequence of the exploitation of man by man. History is its result.

Here, as we saw, economic conditions determine man's behaviour. This leads, by logical necessity, to the creation of ever-newer systems of production leading, in turn, to new economic conditions and the worsening misery of the exploited. But here, too, *redemption* intervenes. With the advent of the capitalist system, the misery of the exploited reaches its peak. It becomes *unbearable*. Then the proletarians become conscious of their condition, and this redemptive consciousness leads to the organization of communist parties, much as Jesus' Resurrection led to the Communion of Saints.

Communist parties wage apocalyptic war against the exploiters. Difficult though this may be, they must necessarily be victorious (this is the 'meaning of history'). Classes will be abolished and man's alienation will end, making way for the establishment of an immutable and classless communist society. And of course, since history is the result of class-struggle, there will be no more history. Prehistoric communism will be restored but sublimated, as the Garden of Eden is restored by the Kingdom of Heaven. While primitive communist societies were afflicted by material misery, post-historical society will enjoy the satisfaction of its needs in perfect equilibrium.

Thus, in the Marxist vision, history is assigned an equally negative value. Born of man's original alienation, it only has a meaning inasmuch as, by endlessly worsening the misery of the exploited, it ultimately creates the conditions of this misery's alleviation, 'working,' in a sense, towards its own end.

Historical Determinism

These two egalitarian visions of history, religious and Christian, secular and Marxist, are both segmental, both eschatological, and logically imply a historical *determinism* which is the doing not of man but of something transcending him. Neither Christianity nor Marxism attempt to deny it. Christians grant man free will in order to blame Adam solely for his error, that is, his imperfection, having freely 'chosen' to sin; but it was still God who made (and thus willed) him imperfect.

Marxists, meanwhile, sometimes say that man makes history, or, more precisely, man as a member of a social class; but social classes are still determined by economic conditions; and it was his original misery that compelled man to start along the bloody trail of class-struggle. Man, then, is simply *directed* by his economic conditions. He is the puppet of circumstances that originate in nature itself, understood as the play of material forces. From which it follows that, while man has a part to play in egalitarian visions of history, it is a part in a drama he has not written, which he cannot have written; and the drama in question is a tragic, shameful, bloody farce. Dignity, man's authentic truth, is found outside history, before and after history.

Everything carries its own relative antithesis *in itself*. The equally egalitarian relative antithesis of the eschatological vision of history is the theory of *infinite progress*. According to this theory, historical movement tends constantly towards a zero-point which is never attained. This 'progress' may head in an 'ever-better' direction, but excludes the notion of a perfect and absolute good. American ideology's *naïve* vision of the 'American way of life' is a little like this, as is a certain disillusioned kind of Marxism. It might also head in an 'ever-worse' direction, the degree of evil never quite reaching its peak. A pessimism of this kind is found in Freud, who did not see how the 'sickness' called civilization could ever cease to reproduce itself. (Note that this pessimistic Freudian vision is currently being assimilated, notably by Marcuse and the Freudo-Marxists, into Marxist eschatology, playing the same part played by every antithesis since Satan — the stooge.)

Animating a New Will

Friedrich Nietzsche, as everyone knows, traced the origins of Christianity, democratic ideology and communism to a common denominator: egalitarianism. But Nietzsche also outlined a second vision of history which opposes the segmental, eschatological vision of contemporary egalitarianism (sometimes covertly, but with all the more tenacity). Indeed, Nietzsche wanted to *combat* egalitarianism as well as to analyse it. He wanted to inspire, to provoke a *project* opposed to the egalitarian project, to animate another will, to reinforce a diametrically opposite value-judgement.

Two complementary aspects of this effort are present in his work. The first is critical, even *scientific*. Its purpose is to show the relativity of all value-judgements, all morals and, therefore, of all purportedly absolute truths. He thereby unmasks the relativity of the principles egalitarianism declares absolute. But beyond this critical aspect there is another, which we might call *poetic*, since this word derives from the Greek *poiein*, meaning 'to do,' 'to create.' Through his poetic efforts, Nietzsche strives to give birth to a new type of man adhering to new values and drawing the principles of his action from an ethic beyond Good and Evil, an ethic we may fairly call 'superhumanist.'

To give a taste of a human society founded on the principles he proposes, Nietzsche almost always takes archaic Greek or the earliest Roman societies as his examples, or even the ancestral societies of the aristocratic and conquering Indo-European 'blond beast.' That much is well-known. But too little attention is paid to the fact that Nietzsche guards against any illusions of 'reviving the Greeks,' that is, of reconstituting the ancient, pre-Christian world. This is an extremely important detail, because it provides a key to understanding the Nietzschean vision of history. Nietzsche went out of his way to hide, we might say 'code,' the organizing system of his thinking. He did so, as he states expressly, in conformity with a certain aristocratic sentiment: he wanted to keep intruders from his door.[2] Therefore, he was content to give us every element of his conception of history without ever showing how one should fit them together.

Moreover, Nietzsche's language is drawn from the *language of myth*, only adding to the interpretative challenges. The thesis defended here is no more than one possible interpretation of the Nietzschean myth of history; but it is an interpretation with good historical grounds, since it inspires whole metapolitical movement of tremendous consequence, that is, the *conservative revolution*; and it is also the interpretation of those who follow Nietzsche most closely in his declaredly anti-egalitarian intentions.

There are three principle elements or mythemes of the Nietzschean vision of history: the *last man*, the advent of the *superman* and, finally, the *Eternal Return* of the Identical.

---

2   *The Gay Science*, 381. — Tr.

The Eternal Return

For Nietzsche, the *last man* is mankind's greatest threat. The last man belongs to the inextinguishable race of midgets. He aspires to a meagre happiness, the same for everyone. He desires the end of history because history is the genetrix of *events*, of conflicts and tensions that imperil his 'meagre happiness.' He mocks Zarathustra, who preaches the advent of the *superman*. For Nietzsche, man is just the 'bridge between beast and superman.'[3] Man and history, then, only have a *meaning* inasmuch as they tend towards an *overcoming* and do not hesitate to accept their own disappearance to this end. The superman is a goal, a goal present at every moment and which may be possible to attain. Or, rather, a goal which, once attained, reappears on the next horizon. From this perspective, history becomes the perpetual overcoming of man by man.

However, there is another element to Nietzsche's vision which seems, at a glance, to contradict the mytheme of the superman, and that is the Eternal Return. Nietzsche does indeed say that the Eternal Return of the Identical governs historical becoming, which seems, at a glance, to imply that nothing new can occur, and that any overcoming is precluded. The theme of the Eternal Return has in fact been read as a cyclical conception of history, strongly recalling that of pagan Antiquity. This is a grave error, in our view, and one against which Nietzsche himself warned. When Zarathustra interrogates the Spirit of Heaviness regarding the two paths that come from opposite directions to join at the gate named 'This Moment,' the Spirit of Heaviness replies: 'Everything straight lieth; all truth is crooked; time itself is a circle.' To which Zarathustra thunderously responds: 'Do not take it too lightly!'[4]

In the Nietzschean vision of history, and unlike the ancient pagan, instants are not understood as successive points on a line, either straight or circular. To understand the basis of the Nietzschean conception is

---

3 *Thus Spake Zarathustra*, 'Zarathustra's Prologue,' 4. — Tr.
4 Ibid., 'The Vision and the Enigma.' — Tr.

historical time, we must compare it to the relativist conception of the four-dimensional physical universe. As we know, the Einsteinian universe cannot be represented 'sensible,' since our sensation, being of a biological order, can only represent three-dimensionally. Similarly, in the Nietzschean historical universe, man's becoming is understood as an ensemble of moments, each of which forms a *sphere* within a four-dimensional 'supersphere' *where, therefore, every moment can occupy the centre with respect to the rest*. In this vision, a moment's actuality is no longer called 'present.' On the contrary, past, present and future coexist at every moment. They are the three dimensions of *every historical moment*. As Zarathustra's birds sing to their master: 'Every moment beginneth existence, around every "Here" rolleth the ball "There." The middle is everywhere. Crooked is the path of eternity.'[5]

The Decision Offered to Our Age

This may all seem rather complicated, much as the theory of relativity itself is 'complicated.' Let us refer to some images for help. For Nietzsche, the past is not what was *once and for all*, something fixed in perpetuity, left behind by the present. Similarly, the future is not an inevitable consequence of every cause preceding and determining it, as in linear conceptions of history. At history's every moment, at every 'actuality,' past and future are, so to speak, *called into question*, formed by a new perspective, forming a *new truth*. Taking another image, we might say that the past is simply the project to which man conforms his historical action, a project he seeks to realize in accordance with an image he makes himself, which he strives to incarnate. So the past reappears as a *prefiguration of the future*. It is, in the true sense of the word, the future's 'imagination.' This is one meaning of the mytheme of the Eternal Return.

It is therefore clear that, in the vision Nietzsche offers us, man bears the whole responsibility for historical becoming. History is *his doing*. Which is to say that he bears the whole responsibility for himself, that

---

5   Ibid., 'The Convalescent.' — Tr.

he is truly and totally free, *faber suae fortunae*. This is an *authentic* freedom, not a 'freedom' conditioned by Grace or material, economic conditions. It is also *real* freedom, that is, a freedom to decide between two opposites, given at every moment in history, and calling the totality of man's being and becoming into question. (Unless these choices are *always realizable*, this is a false choice, a false freedom, and man's autonomy mere make-believe.)

Now, what decision is presented to men of our age? The decision, Nietzsche says, is between the 'last man,' that is, the man of the *end of history*, and the urge towards the superman, that is, the *regeneration of history*. For Nietzsche, these two options are as real as they are fundamental. He affirms that the end of history is *possible*, that it must be seriously contemplated, just as the opposite, the regeneration of history, is *possible*. Ultimately, it falls to men, to the decision they make between these two camps: the egalitarian movement, which Nietzsche called the movement of the last man, and another movement, which Nietzsche strives to muster, which he has already mustered, and which he calls his own.

Two Sensibilities

A *linear* vision and a *spherical* vision. We are faced with two sensibilities which have always opposed, and will always oppose one another. These two sensibilities cohabit the present age. The egalitarian sensibility can only see the Pyramids, for example, as an execrable symbol from the moral perspective, since only slavery, the exploitation of man by man, could permit one to conceive and realize these monuments. The other sensibility, however, would first be smitten by the *uniqueness* of this architectural and artistic expression, by all it considers great and terrible in the man who dares to make history, who desires to equal his destiny.

Let us take another example. In a famous passage, Oswald Spengler remembers that Roman sentinel from Pompeii who let himself be entombed by cinders because no superior had relieved him of his post.⁶ For the egalitarian sensibility bound to a segmental vision of history, such a tale is utterly bereft of *meaning*. Ultimately, it can only condemn it, just as it condemns history, since, so far as it is concerned, that soldier was the victim of an illusion or a 'pointless' error. But inversely, the same gesture *immediately* becomes exemplary from the superhumanist point of view, which understands, we might say intuitively, that this soldier only truly reached manhood by conforming to the image, which he himself has fashioned, of a sentinel of the Imperial City.

We cited Spengler. This leads us to follow him in asking the question of the destiny of the West. Spengler, as we know, was a pessimist. For him, the West's end is night, and there is nothing for European man to do but *do his bit* to its bitter end, where he shall die a tragic hero in the conflagration of his world and civilization. But today, in 1975, the West is heading towards the end of history, full stop. She begs to return to the immobile happiness of the species and sees nothing tragic in this prospect. Quite the contrary. The egalitarian, universalist West is ashamed of her past. She is horrified by the very uniqueness that secured her superiority throughout the centuries that she followed, subconsciously, an ethic she had given herself.

For this two-thousand-year-old West is also a Judaeo-Christian West which has, at last, *discovered itself as such* and is now reaping the consequences. Of course, the same West enjoyed a Greek, Celtic, Germanic, Roman heritage from which it drew its strength. But Western masses, lacking true masters, deny this Indo-European heritage. Only small minorities, scattered here and there, survey the achievements of their most distant ancestors with nostalgia, inspired by their values which they dream of reviving. These minorities may seem desultory; and perhaps they are. But a minority, however minuscule, may always attain the value of a mass. And so the modern West,

---

6   *Man and Technics*, tr. C. F. Anderson (New York: Alfred A. Knopf, 1943), p. 104. — Tr.

the West born of the Constantinian compromise and the *In hoc signo vinces*, has turned schizophrenic. By an immense majority, she longs for the end of history and hopes to find happiness in regression. But at the same time, small minorities strive to found a new aristocracy and hope for a Return, which can never occur as such ('We cannot revive the Greeks'), but which might metamorphose into a regeneration of history.

Towards a Regeneration of History

Those who take a linear or segmental view of history feel sure they are on the side of the angels, as some say, or the right side of history, as others say. Their adversaries? They *cannot be certain*. Believing that history is made by man and by man alone, that man is free, and free to forge his own destiny, they must admit that this same freedom is, ultimately, the freedom to imperil or even to abolish man's historicity. They must think the end of history possible, let us repeat, even if they reject this possibility and struggle against it. But if the end of history is possible, so is the regeneration of history, and at any moment. Because history is neither a reflection of divine will nor the result of economically determined class-struggle, but, rather, the struggle among men in the name of images they themselves make and which they mean, by realizing, to equal.

In the age in which we live, some only find meaning in history to the extent that it tends towards the negation of man's historical condition. For others, history's meaning is none other than the meaning of a certain image of man, an image used and consumed by the march of historical time. An image fashioned in the past, but which still forms their present. An image which can only be realized through the regeneration of historical time. They know the West is a pile of ruins. But, like Nietzsche, they also know that stars are born from dark and swirling clouds of dust.

The author wrote this article, which appeared in *Nouvelle École* (no. 20, September–October 1972), essentially for his readers in France, where 'nationalist' is an adjective by which a whole political grouping is defined, and defines itself. (Despite the insistent usage of the term 'national' by certain post-war political circles, nationalism has not existed in Giorgio Locchi's Italian homeland since at least 1945. In Germany and Austria, to a certain extent, it may have ceased to exist before even that date. Italy has seen patriotic positions, which have recently become as dominant as transversal, including among the government elected in 2022, but which are a quite different thing.) The appearance of this text in Italy in *L'Uomo libero* (no. 9) ten years later, as well as the brief career of Francesco Bergomi's journal *Estera*, also contributed, by dissipating certain misunderstandings, to the conditions of a fusion of an identitarian character between the most developed parts of ethno-regionalism and so-called 'European nationalism,' aiming at an organizational model different from those of the centralist and Jacobin nation-states which, since the second half of the twentieth century, denounced, as much in Western as in Eastern Europe, the total exhaustion of their forward momentum and a worsening crisis of sovereignty. This line of thinking, among others, would leave one of the most durable traces of Locchi's thinking on the New Right, which would never deny it. See what Alain de Benoist was still writing in *L'Empire intérieur* (1996) and *Identité et communauté* (2005).

3

Kingdom, Empire, *Imperium*

IT CAN HARDLY be too often repeated that there are two ways of 'feeling,' of unconsciously conceiving the *nation*, two ways that follow from the dichotomy that characterizes the history of Western Europe. If we agree to understand the nation as a community founded on (and by) language, civilization and 'destiny' (though we shall define the concept better later on), then we see at once that, in France's case, the *nation* is born from the laborious efforts of the *state* ('forty kings…'), while, in Germany's or Italy's cases, the *state* was the realization, the 'translation' into political terms, of a late-dawning *national consciousness*. We might call this a 'nation-cause,' as opposed to a 'nation-effect.'

In this Hexagon, whose rough outlines were first traced by Roman administrators, very diverse populations (in terms of race, language, custom, civilization) have been overlaid and thrown together, since the collapse of that empire. Recall that, in the same period, the concept *gentes* proved insufficient to discern new ethnopolitical realities, gradually ceding its place to the concept *nationes*.

Everyone knows that one of the Hexagon's 'nations,' the Frankish, would go on to *reduce* and *assimilate* the rest by imposing its language, law and civilization, sometimes by force. This process of assimilation was not accomplished without 'upset'; and this is still palpable in the 'French' political atmosphere today. It is still clear, whether we like it or not, that the ancient non-Frankish 'nations' have lost even their potential *vis politica*, and even where they survive in quite lively *folkloric* expressions. In fact, autonomist groups cannot *imagine* their ethnicities' autonomy in a scenario in which existing states still exist (that is, the contemporary *international* political order): so they are compelled to project their ideal onto a future scenario, sometimes European ('Europeanist'), sometimes universal (universalist). They therefore recognize, though often not quite consciously, that they cannot truly *differentiate*, that is, *separate* themselves from France except in a world in which there is no France, nor, for that matter, an England, Italy, Germany, Belgium or Netherlands (a sentiment we may take to prove the healthiness of the instincts, and the political realism, of at least some of these groups).

Italians and Germans

Turning now to the cases of Germany and Italy, we find a thoroughly different historical panorama, whose characteristic facts are opposite to those of the French case (or the English, or even Spanish; though there are also important variations here).

Somehow, the Frankish kings 'overturned' the Roman political heritage. Separating from the Empire in 843 (signing of the Treaty of Verdun), they also rejected the imperial *idea*, aiming instead at the *reduction* of the Hexagon's ethnopolitical realities to the Frankish model. Which was what we might call *regnum*, political power no longer *organized* by nation (as under the Empire) but by *class*, derived, more or less, from 'nations,' of course, but which would very quickly forget this fact. Beyond the Vosges, meanwhile, among the *Teutschen*, the idea of *imperium* stayed in circulation and continued to haunt minds and dominate every political endeavour. This idea, it must be said, was still utterly unrealistic. The German Holy Roman Empire (*Heiliges Römisches Reich Deutscher Nation*) was little more than the appearance of itself; though the imperial idea was still powerful enough to impose a 'structure' which became the very destiny of the peoples that followed it. *Nations* formed in its midst, derived from former *nationes*; but they could never achieve genuine political consciousness while the imperial idea inherited from Rome opposed it.[1] Similarly, Dante, for whom the *Italian* was a linguistic and civilizational fact, cried out to the *veltro* (the *dux*), that is, for the Holy Roman Emperor, who was German. As a Ghibelline, politically opposed to the Guelfs, the Florentine Dante saw in his Pisan neighbours the *vituperio delle genti* ('the opprobrium of the people'). For him, Italy was simply 'the fair land where the "*sì*" [the "yes"] doth sound.'[2] At that time, then, there was not *a* Germany or *an* Italy but *Italians* and *Germans*.

For Italian of German political *national consciousness* to emerge, it was necessary that the imperial 'appearance' fade away. And that is what happened, slowly and imperceptibly, at the hands of History, who is always brutal to those who insist upon a dream. The Thirty Years' War, the series of foreign dominations that turned Italy into a humiliated and bloody battlefield, marked the climax of this process. But that was still insufficient. It was also necessary that everything *linked by opposition* to the Empire should crumble and disappear: first of all its *internal antithesis*, the Catholic Church; but also its external antithesis, the *Kingdom*. This was brought about by the Revolution of 1789, which was the culmination of a peculiarly French process of political evolution, and then Romanticism, which, on the contrary, reacted against the diffusion of revolutionary ideas (in Germany, at least).

'Forty Kings'

Born from the absolute negation of the idea of Empire, the Kingdom of France asserted the supremacy of one *natio* over the rest, implicitly and in fact. At the beginning, a feudal aristocracy of Germanic origin

---

1 After the fall of Rome, the idea of Empire was swept up by a new dialectic. The temporal Empire was opposed (though in itself *indissolubly linked*) to the idea of spiritual Empire. The temporal Empire was *holy* and Christian; the spiritual Empire was *Roman* and Catholic. We shall not discuss this dialectic or its evolution, which fall beyond our present scope.

2 *Inferno*, 33.79–80. — Tr.

played a role analogous to that of the Roman *gens* in the birth of the *civitas*. But since it *did not express* sovereign power, this aristocracy lost, little by little, its ethnic form and historical consciousness. This happened in a rather complex way. The Frankish aristocracy found it necessary to assimilate the aristocracies of other *nationes* within the Hexagon. Now, these aristocracies expressed centrifugal tendencies opposed to the royal task of centralization. Therefore, the kings were compelled to combat the aristocratic class, or at least to oppose some of its pretensions, even though this class had originally been one of the bases of royal power. Everyone knows the result. Once Louis XIV had stripped the aristocracy of its powers, having *bled* it of its political significance, thus transforming it into a parasitical political class by means of the seductions of the gilded cage that was the Court of Versailles, the Revolution was inevitable. This Revolution was essentially anti-aristocratic, rather than anti-monarchical, to the extent that it would be no exaggeration to say that the '*grands ancêtres*' of 1789 did nothing more than carry a process, which the 'Forty Kings' had set in motion in centuries past, through to its conclusion.[3]

Once the amalgam that was the French nation came into being, the French Revolution acknowledged that the privilege class had lost its *justification* along with its *responsibilities*. Thus arose the concept of the *nation-state*, which would impose itself upon the minds of European peoples in the course of the Revolutionary Wars. Once formed or, more precisely, created by the state (by *a* state), the French "nation" could now assert its ownership over this state. This was the French *Republic*.

Faced with this French nation (and all the more once she became conqueress under Napoleon), the peoples of Europe recognized

---

3 The revolutionaries of 1789 only turned on Louis XIV once it became clear that he would refuse to 'play the game,' and that, understanding nothing of his ancestors' policy, he sided with the *Versaillaise* aristocracy, rather than continuing to invest in the bourgeoisie. Whence the disillusioned judgement of Bonaparte, who, seeing the toppled sovereign pass by, shouted: '*Coglione!*'

themselves as *nations* and desired, quite naturally, to express their own *state*. In Germany and Italy, this political movement towards 'independence' and 'national unification' was entangled, at the level of ideas, with Romanticism. Except, since their historical inheritance was entirely different from France's, Italian and German Romantics conceived the *nation*, and this nation's right to express itself as a *state*, in a form radically opposed to the French. There was certainly a *current* within (German and Italian) Romanticism that accepted French ideas as they were (that is, as more or less consciously expressing a Christian, egalitarian will). It is not this current we shall discuss here, of course, but the more authentically Italian or German Romanticism whence these peoples' 'parallel destiny' flowed, until the first half of the present century.

The Romantic 'Nation'

The *nation* conceived by the French Revolution is a fundamentally democratic, fundamentally egalitarian and 'anti-classist' nation, even if its egalitarianism and 'anti-classism' appear only in law, as a sort of *negative relief*.[4] On the other hand, the 'Romantic' nation (taking the term in the restricted sense specified above) is neither egalitarian nor democratic. According to 'revolutionary' logic, one nation (any nation) is equal in right to another (every other). But this is not so in the Italian or German Romantic conception, where even language itself tries to express this difference (where the French speak of the *nation*, the Germans speak rather of the *Volk*, and certain Italians of the *popolo*). Thus, Vincenzo Gioberti loudly proclaims *il primato degli Italiani* ('the primacy of the Italians'), while Johann Gottlieb Fichte extols the *uniqueness* of the German people, the lone *Volk* in a world of mere masses.

---

4 However, in this respect, the destiny of the now purely economic *class* is distinguished from that of the *family* and blood. The individual is *monadized*.

This is easily explained. In the Hexagon, the shift from the idea of empire to that of the kingdom amounted, in fact, to a contraction of the geographical horizon. The necessary result of this inward turn was '*France seule*' ['France alone']. And this turn also necessitated that, sooner or later, the equality of other nations, of the Other *tout court*, be recognized. In contrast, fidelity to the idea of empire requires the conception of a genuine 'political cosmos' encompassing all peoples within a hierarchical organization.

At the very moment national consciousness made its bloody entrance into European history, Ludwig van Beethoven shattered the spirit of his age by composing his marvellous Ninth Symphony, a hymn to the joy of all mankind, whose history has just become global. Once Bonaparte gave way to Napoleon, the same Beethoven scrubbed out the dedication to his *Eroica*; though he was nevertheless utterly incapable of imagining this song of the reconciliation of peoples assembling in the new cosmos without some coryphaeus to rouse them, to conduct and organize them. At this point, let us recall the 'two enemy souls' inextricably interwoven in the Romantic breast…

Indo-Europeans

Let us return to the Roman idea of the *imperium* and to its political translation. Early Indo-European societies, as far as we can understand them through comparative study, display a strange contrast between the severe discipline exercised within the basic socio-political cell, the 'extended family', the clan, and, on the other hand, the markedly anarchic tendency of the *relations* between cells. In fact, this contrast, which is closely linked to the dynamic of Indo-European history, only appears strange from the *modern* perspective. The socio-political reality of the remote age in which the Indo-Europeans entered History (the beginning of the Neolithic) is that of a restricted group: the *clan*. And relations between clans were of much the same nature as those between *cities* or *states* in other eras. Whence the quite illusory impression of 'anarchy' one might get when one examines the ethnic unity of the Indo-Europeans or seeks to understand *their* society. Now, there never was *an* Indo-European society. The Indo-Europeans never imagined any grand socio-political unity for the good reason that they were not (and could not have been) conscious of what *unites* them in our eyes.

The Indo-Europeans could only become conscious of this gradually, when, in later ages, they left their isolation and were confronted by *other* ethnicities, *other* civilizations. Moreover, this was not easily attained, and almost never completely. The great 'super-tribal' confederations that formed with migratory expeditions and the first settlements in new lands and amongst new peoples were generally short-lived and tended to dissolve. The establishment of *royal power*, which, in the beginning, simply ensured the organization and discipline of the *horde* during the process of its relocation (with king being 'the one who knows which path to follow'), initially had a simply electoral and provisional character. Since it tended by its very nature to consolidate itself and become hereditary, it always met with resistance from clan-chiefs once a conquest was achieved. Therefore, the earliest histories of those Indo-European groups that moved into new territories were bound up in the gradual degradation of monarchical authority and the 're-atomization' of the group. This was especially the case among the Greeks and Celts.

Elsewhere, the institutionalization of royalty was achieved, but at the expense of an entire Indo-European (cultural but also genetic) tradition. So it was with the people of Nessa, who lost their name and became the Hittites, and with certain Germanic peoples who ran aground on Mediterranean shores.

In Capital Letters

The Indo-European peoples were well aware, in a general way, of the necessity of preserving their originality while accepting the consequences of the gradual triumph of the 'Neolithic Revolution' and the widening of cultural and geopolitical horizons that it imposed upon them. But (keeping to the ancient world) only the Romans achieved a synthesis of perennity, fidelity to themselves and to their origins, and a full and unqualified acceptance of their 'cosmic entanglement.' This synthesis took a name which would be engraved upon History in capital letters: *imperium*.

So let us examine it. The idea of *imperium* must not be confused with that of empire, even of the Roman Empire. Indeed, there can be no doubt that the truth and the most perfect realization of *imperium* was found in the *effort to construct* Republican Rome, rather than in the *effort to maintain* the post-Julian Empire. *Imperium* expresses a will to cosmic order; and this is the order that organizes the *gentes* hierarchically. Therefore, in theory and in practice, *imperium* stands at the antipode of every 'universalism.' It does not try to reduce *kinds* of men to one and the same *mankind*, but endeavours, on the contrary, to preserve differences in a world given necessarily to unification. The Romans simply wished to preserve their own *city*, their own *ius* (since, by nature, they understood everything in terms of rite and law). But at home, this will to authenticity logically entailed the *recognition of the Other*. It was in this that their political greatness consisted — of which, parenthetically, they were always well aware. And one might almost call Rome's *conquering* endeavours mere 'by-products' of another, purely defensive endeavour. After all, one must never forget that the word *urbs* derives from an Indo-European root originally meaning a 'refuge protected by water.'

History as Destiny

In a world in which peoples were forced by the 'Neolithic Revolution' out of isolation and into a complex network of increasingly direct relationships, the Roman *imperium* represented the gradual enlargement of the protective enclosure of the *urbs*. It was the rampart behind which the *civis romanus* was able to live to its own rhythm and under its own law, precisely to the extent that, according to a logic of franchise, the rest enjoyed the same guarantee.

Nonetheless, as an active and thoroughgoing rejection of every *universalism*, of every reduction *ad unum*, *imperium* is political, that is, realist, and not utopian. It is hierarchical. Therein, everyone retains his own *ius*, his own law; every people is free to administer its city according to its traditional justice. But in relations between persons from different cities, or between the cities themselves, Roman *ius* always precedes Latin *ius*, which precedes all the rest. And where neither Roman nor Latin *ius* is involved, the *ius gentium* is applied, a rather Roman abstraction, meant to correspond to what is common to the *iura* of all peoples. Therefore, under the *imperium*, Rome enjoyed absolute supremacy, explained quite naturally and in perfect justice by the fact that she conceived and created, organized and ensured this order under which each receives the due apportioned him by History, that is, by *fatum*.

The Greeks, *dreaming* like artists, had also tried to synthesize fidelity to what they were with the fatal exigencies of their engagement with a 'wider' world…but widened only to the limits of Hellenism. Therefore, they were compelled to 'domesticate' war, ritualizing natural aggression through an *agon* (contest) encompassing every aspect of civic life in the *polis*. With the Olympiads, they wished to ensure a Pan-Hellenic *order*, at least periodically. And the peace imposed by that order sprang, very significantly, from the triumphal staging of *agon*.

Rome lived the Hellenic dream and brought it alive for the *whole world*. The Romans did not 'domesticate' war. Quite to the contrary, they institutionalized it, knowing that war is just one of the spectacles constantly recurring under the gaze of the *bifrons* god. And *peace* was also institutionalized (*pax romana*). It no longer supervened on the 'domestication' of war into a game, but supervened, *within* imperium, *on the order arising from war*, and also on the principle of perpetual war between those within *imperium* and those not yet within it. And since *imperium* represents order consecrated by *fatum*, many peoples ended up appealing to the Romans and begging admission to the Empire (if only to try to withdraw once their affairs were satisfactorily arranged: take the Gauls, who appealed to Rome against the Germans, then rebelled unsuccessfully against an order to which they themselves had resorted).

'*Tu regere imperio populos, Romane, memento... Parcere subiectis, et debellare superbos*': This is the definition proposed by the Gaulish poet Virgil of the mission the Romans had given themselves.[5] So just a definition is it that, after Rome had fallen, the peoples of Europe retained a nostalgia for Roman order and tried, vainly and by any means, to restore it. Rome thus became synonymous with 'political order'; and the name 'Caesar,' *imperator* par excellence, was given to bearers of sovereign power charged with ensuring order.

The Last Roman

Some might object that, in fact, the *imperium* gave rise to the very universalism, the very ethnic chaos is meant to preclude, and that it was unable to maintain itself for the centuries prior to its deterioration and disappearance. '*Orbis fecisti quod prius Urbis erat*,' sang another Gaulish poet, Rutilius Namatianus, who lived under Honorius.[6] The poet was correct; but we should add that Rome never desired it. Everything in History has its day. Nothing there is eternal or absolute. It is always a matter of bending History to a will, of striving to give it a *form*. Within the span of History they lived to see, the Romans asserted themselves over and against all, realizing the only project of *imperium* ever yet to exist. They maintained it *as long as they lasted*.

---

[5] Drawn from the following verses: '*Tu regere imperio populos, Romane, memento; | Hae tibi erunt artes; pacisque imponere morem, | Parcere subiectis, et debellare superbos.*' 'Be thy charge, O Roman, to rule the nations in thine *imperium*; this shall be thine art, to lay down the law of peace, to be merciful to the conquered and beat the haughty down.' Virgil, *Aeneid*, VI.853-6 (tr. J. W. Mackail). — Ed. [Footnotes marked with "Ed." are by the French editor of the original.]

[6] 'Thou hast made a city of what was erstwhile a world': from Rutilius Namatianus's poem *Iter Maritimum*, I, 63-6 (tr. J. W. and A. M. Duff), the last *homage* to Rome's greatness. — Ed.

For the *imperium* only really began to deteriorate when there were no more Romans; when 'Rome was no longer in Rome.'[7] Perhaps it was not immediately noticed that the last descendants of the *gentes* were dead on the battlefield. Or perhaps it was. But it was carefully hidden. To all appearances, those who then called themselves Romans were believed to be Romans in fact. The last of the Romans himself likely knew who he was. He was not ignorant that 'tomorrow' was a pious fiction, and could laugh after his own fashion: cruel, sovereignly disdainful, and nonetheless compassionate. Perhaps, when he elevated his horse to the dignity of senator or consul, he wished quietly to make it known that, once there were no more genuine Romans, anyone and everyone would become Roman…

Imperial Order

With the Industrial Revolution, mankind has now entered a period of *globalization*. No people can excuse itself from this global situation or afford to dream of some impossible isolation. Global order is compulsory. Sooner or later, it is *fatal*. Tomorrow's great politics can only be understood and enacted as taking what Ernst Jünger called the *Weltstaat*, the global state, as motive and end. The symptoms are already evident: the League of Nations and then the United nations, by way of utopia; the Soviet empire and the American empire, in reality. But nothing should lead one to believe that the United States are any more capable than the Soviet Union of becoming tomorrow's Rome. These 'blocs,' which seek to organize optimally the tools made available by the Industrial Revolution, more readily recall Pharaonic Egypt or the successive theocracies of the Fertile Crescent… Nevertheless, it remains the case that the globalization now under way requires *cosmic order*. Is this order to be 'imperial' or, contrarily, 'republican' (in the French sense of the term), that is, egalitarian? None can say: for the history of the future is open. We can only move in one direction or

---

7   See Pierre Corneille, *Sertorius*, 3.1. — Tr.

the other. The egalitarian solution culminating in a universal 'republic' entails the reduction of mankind *ad unum*, uniformization and the generation of a 'universal type.' The 'imperial' solution, let us repeat, is hierarchical. If *freedom*, according to egalitarian dialectic, is one *absolute* opposed to another (the negation of freedom), in 'imperial' dialectic, it is *relative* and bound to the idea of social responsibility. Under *imperium*, it is the right of the better, according to the *virtue* of his age, that is absolute. But *imperium* is also the only means to preserve differences within (and through) a global situation, according to the principle of *uniquique suum*, implicitly recognizing the basic fact of the diversity of values.

From the strictly psychological perspective, the aversion of certain autonomists (or ethnicists) from the egalitarian idea of the 'republic' is perfectly justified. But they seriously mislead themselves if they imagine the substitution of the extant with a 'universalist' order would suffice to solve their problems. For the 'Republic' conceived by the men of 1789 is simply a foreshadow, at the *national* level, of a *global* egalitarian state still more reductive and levelling than the Jacobins ever were.

This text is in fact Giorgio Locchi's final contribution to GRECE's annual colloquium, from 1979. Indeed, it was around this time that the terms 'myth' and 'community,' understood in a somewhat different way to the usual, gained more and more popularity in many European circles — and that was certainly not unrelated to the rediscovery around that time of Ferdinand Tönnies. With his habitual concision, Locchi indicates how they ought to be used and what we ought to think of them.

4

Myth and Community

FRIEDRICH NIETZSCHE foresaw almost every characteristic phenomenon of our age a good century in advance: the upsurge of anarchistic nihilism, the epidemic of neuroses, the remarkable ascendency of showbusiness debased to the level of everyday '*circenses*,' the trade in self-indulgence. This vindication of Nietzschean prophecy ought to strike the mind, provoke it to contemplation. This has not happened. But that was fated. Nietzsche diagnosed Western societies with decadence and simply foresaw the normal progression of the sickness. Now, one effect of the social sickness called decadence is the sufferer's blindness regarding his own condition. The sicker he grows, the healthier he thinks himself. So, the nearer a decadent society comes to its sickness' fatal end, the more progressivist it becomes.

Look around. Everyone, from the more or less advanced liberal to the more or less retarded communist, believes viscerally in progress, thoroughly convinced that he lives in an are of progress, even the heights of progress. He surveys all kinds of phenomena which, in the long history of peoples, have always characterized a people's or a culture's final agonies. From feminism to the glittering rise of minstrels and theatrical types; from the disintegration of traditional social nuclei — in our case, families — to ephemeral but tireless attempts to replace them with some kind of commune or other; from masochistic universalism to the collapse of all individually restrictive social norms.

But he is utterly incapable of learning history's lesson, which sometimes leads him to suppose that history has no meaning.

Another characteristic of advanced decadence is mediocrity of feeling. We squabble spitefully but tolerate one another. We still make war, cold if possible, but in love's name, in order to liberate the other. We oblige ourselves to hate an abstraction of the other, but never the reality of the other. Depending on the wing we occupy, we hate wicked Western capitalism or the beastly communist regime, but we love the Russian people or the good old American people. Decadent societies forget how to love and hate. They turn tepid as life deserts them; their vital force has all but dissipated. This vital force, which enlivens societies, organizes them and sets them on history's perilous path, goes by many names. Dostoyevsky called it God, and said that, once a people loses its God, it can only agonize and die. Friedrich Nietzsche announced to Western societies that their God was dead and that they themselves would therefore die. Paul Valéry sensed the same truth in his own way. For me, 'God' is too tight, to Western a term for society's vital force. The divine is only an element, an aspect of that vital force which I would rather call, in all its complexity, Myth.

Myth, as I understand it, enters history to create itself, creating and organizing its own elements. Myth is that historical force which enlivens a community, organizes it, launches it upon its destiny. Myth is, first of all, a world-feeling, but a shared world-feeing and, as such, objective, creating both social bonds and communal norms. It structures a community, styles its life, and also structures individual personalities. These world-feeling also originates a worldview and, therefore, coherent expressions of thought. History shows that each people, each civilization has its own Myth. From the perspective of contemporary society, we get the impression that Myths always belong to a primordial phase of human development which is now closed. That Myth belongs to mankind's infancy is a commonplace of modern historical reflection. But this thought is the inevitable reflection of a civilization's senescence. Once a Myth is dead and we examine it from without, it appears to be an assemblage of more or less delusive beliefs, a collection of fantastical tales, strangely confused, invariably contradictory. If one tries to relate a Myth, after the fact, to life or history, it seems to move against the current of one's time, which led Mircea Eliade to say that Myth is a nostalgia for origins. But he found that one cannot study life with a corpse. A living Myth is recognizable by its harmony and fusion of opposites. This is simply to say that men who life within a Myth's sphere of influence and who are organized by it do not experience as contradictory what seems contradictory from without. Myth is a living, creative force; and it proves itself such by its creativity, which indefatigably resolves contradictions. There was once a name for this resolutory power: it was called faith. Rationally, this leads us in a vicious circle, another form of contradiction. Myth is true only in faith; but faith lives only in Myth. Faith is created by Myth alone.

For those within a Myth, this vicious circle, this contradiction, is no such thing: for Myth lives within those it encompasses and is tirelessly created by and between them. Indeed, Myth is the tireless creation of oneself. It is, in every respect, a self-creation. This is true even at the linguistic level, which is the level at which man, as a social being, takes shape. Some illustrious structuralists inform us that one does not speak; that one is 'spoken.' Evidently they speak of and for themselves as eminent representatives of contemporary society. They are not wrong. Any language detached from the Myth — that is, the world-feeling — that created it can only be spoken, in the sense that those who use it do not speak but are spoken. As long as language is vitally attached to its mythic root, it remains in a process of self-creation, and those who use it still speak, and speak one to another, far from any Tower of Babel.

The language of Myth structures symbols. It creates things with words. Once Myth no longer speaks but is, at best, still spoken, symbolic harmony is displaced by the discord of two irreconcilably opposite ideas. This also means, tautologically, that the age of Myth is displaced by the age of ideologies, ideologies which, though springing from one source, are implacably opposed, and which vainly attempt an impossible synthesis in an 'ultimate science' which might recover the lost paradise guaranteed by Myth's harmony.

Since this is a harmony of opposites, Myth is the social bond *par excellence*; and it is legitimate to speak, in this connection, of religion. As a social bond, Myth organizes society, guaranteeing its coherence in space and across time. Myth is more than a *Weltanschauung* (worldview). It is a world-feeling and, at the same time or, better still, by the same token, a value-feeling, an operative measure. It is the key that explains, that suggests an action and the norm of that action. Recall how Myth can organize a society, dictating the conduct of men confronted by an unforeseen problem, in this case the Hellenes. The Greeks were Indo-Europeans; their Myth was the Indo-European Myth on which basis they organized themselves into a patrilineal society founded on what we might call heroic values. When they migrated into the Greek peninsula, they ran into a matrilineal society. For possibly contingent reasons, they did not destroy this society. These peoples, these civilizations intermixed. This posed a grave problem: the irreconcilable opposition of two conceptions of society and of law. In matriarchal societies, women do not make war or hold power but men, as elsewhere. But legitimacy with respect to power passes through the woman. A man cannot rule unless he marry a woman who inherits power by matrilineal right. In such societies, power is always held by men chosen by women. Now, if we are right to consider the Hellenes to have acquired power, at the beginning of this process of intermixture, by virtue of marriage, then they must nonetheless have sought to legitimize this from the perspective of their own Myth, the perspective of patrilineal right. A whole host of mythical tales retell these conflicts and the thousand ways by which the Hellenes ensured their value-system would triumph. The adventures of Oedipus, Orestes, the myths of Theseus, Jason, Bellerophon, even the rape of Europa, are just a few of many examples. And in the Pantheon, which certainly derived from two mythic religions, the supremacy of paternal right is symbolized by Athena, the virgin, warrior goddess, but also the goddess of reflective thought. Athena has no mother; she claims to 'have only a father,' Zeus; and it is she who absolves Orestes who must kill his mother to avenge his father.

The intimate relationship between founding Myth, society, value-system and social norm permits us to speak of society as an organism and of organic society. Moreover, this term, society, is ill-fitting, as our having to qualify it with an adjective demonstrates. So, from now on, I use 'community' to mean organic society, and set community and society against one another, much as one opposes one limit-concept to another. This opposition between community and society is nothing new: it was made by certain German sociologists, notably Ferdinand Tönnies. Their intuition was correct; but they always followed it to erroneous conclusions or muddle theories, since the definition of community, as opposed to society, was only ever made implicitly.

A Myth is always nostalgia for origins, as Mircea Eliade said; but it is also always a cosmological vision of the future. It announces a world's end, which can sometimes become the beginning of that world's repetition or, in one well-known case, its regeneration.

Myth, we also say, has no time. It has none because it is time, historical time. The community it organizes is a historical organism which occupies, at every moment, the three dimensions of historical time. A community is a living organism, occupying past, present and future at once. A community has a common consciousness, which is at once memory, action and project. We call a community of this sort a people. Once a people loses the memory of its origins and, as Richard Wagner says, ceases to be moved by shared passion and suffering, then it is no longer a people. It becomes a mass; and community becomes society. I called community and society limit-concepts. There is always a little of the mass in the best of peoples and a trace of the people in the vilest and most degraded masses. there can be no doubt (after all, it is endlessly repeated) that we live in an age of masses, that we live in massified societies. The individual, whoever he may be, is divinized in the name of equality. Every individual in a society has the same value. On the other hand, in a community, human value, which always means social personality, is measured by its conformity with ideal types proposed by Myth which every member of the community internalizes as a sort of superego. Once Myth disintegrates, once these ideal archetypes are no longer experienced as such, there is no more communal bond, so that, ultimately, every individual is thought to be an ideal in himself by virtue of his mere individuality. Only the ever-precarious and contingent link created by the self-interested alliance of individuals into classes, parties, churches or sects remains to cobble what has become a society together. The authentically human dimension, the historical dimension, is lost. Mass society is no longer concerned with past or future: it lives in and for the present alone. Therefore, it no longer engages in politics: it merely sustains an economy, an economy of the worst kind, at that, which conditions all social reflexes. Symptomatically, a preoccupation with the future, the horizon of the year 2000, is aroused only to justify present economic failure and to make it palatable. Understand that we are speaking only of our Western societies. These societies, in which we are born and live, are derivatives of the great Christian *oecumene*, which was made and moulded by the Judaeo-Christian Myth. This Myth is long dead, and its God with it. Even religion, such as what the tatters of the Church still sustains, is ideologized, becoming just one ideology opposed to countless others flowing from the same mythic spring, now running dry. Where Myth organized, harmonized, united and thereby gave spiritual, that is, human meaning and content to the lives of men, ideologies oppose, disunify, disaggregate. Ideology rejects Myth as irrational and purports itself to be rational and rationally grounded. Fundamentally, every ideology claims, implicitly or explicitly, to be science, moreover the science of man. And in its quest for rationalization, every ideology ends up becoming an anti-ideology. Indeed, since one ideology is never without another, contrary ideology, this rivalry leads to a synthesis in a kind of illusory ideological neutrality sustained by the preposterous conviction that, in the end everything, even man, is quantifiable, that everything is calculable, and that a society's life is reducible to questions of administration.

For example, Western societies imagine they can recover a lost harmony, the intimate fusion of opposites, by means of tolerance; but they thereby turn schizophrenic and render schizophrenic those individuals most sensitive to the social climate. The Western individual will always end up with a bad conscience, most of all when it comes to power, because he is harassed by two contrary needs which cannot simultaneously be justified: let us say, for the sake of simplicity, the need for individual freedom and the need for social justice. This dismemberment of society also affects individuals, sometimes comically, as with advanced liberals who imagine themselves socialists, or communists and socialists who fancy themselves liberals.[1] And remember that when we mock Myth and spurn it as irrational, we will try instinctually to claw back its social benefits by proposing an Antimyth and a corresponding ideal, the Antihero, an ideal ably represented at the level of the mass-consumption of social pseudo-values by the dishevelled artist, long-haired, a little dirty if possible.

Communist societies, also derivatives of the Judaeo-Christian myth, tried another solution. They chose intolerance in favour of a single ideology invoked in place of Myth. But since ideology is not Myth, and cannot operate on the souls of individuals, individuals will never conform to its ideological norm. The well-known consequence is that communist societies are societies of repression. To be precise, at every level of communist societies repression is an obligation, so that the purifier himself becomes purified, while in liberal-democratic societies, toleration is an obligation from which even delinquents benefit. Moreover, despite keeping up certain 'anti-economic' appearances,

---

1   Remember that Locchi's speech here transcribed dates to a decade before the fall of the Berlin Wall. Today, all this is truer than ever, and even taken for granted. — Ed.

communist societies live only in the present. One periodic and striking demonstration is its condemnation of every bygone present, which takes on the aspect of ritual celebration. The present is always divinized, from Lenin to Stalin to Mao, until it cedes its place to another present by which it is infallibly condemned and excommunicated. So, all in all, we might say that the respective social equations of communist and liberal-democratic societies have the same value. Microscopically, at the individual level, liberal society is more attractive, which has led to dissent within and emigration from communist regimes and, in reaction, the Berlin Wall. But note that, at the macroscopic level of the mass as such, the migration has happened in the other direction and, since the War, socialist societies have multiplied.[2]

So, what to do? What to expect? Allow me to return to Nietzsche. Nietzsche was among the first to announce that Western civilization is beginning an agony, an agony of unforeseeable duration, and that she is going to die. European nations are condemned either to exit history, like the Bororós so dear to Mr. Lévi-Strauss, or to perish historically and see their biological substance dissolved into nations and peoples to come. Fundamentally, everyone in Europe more or less knows this; and for this reason, Europe has been a matter of debate for some time. But here Europe is understood to be the prolongation of current social realities, the last chance of saving she who agonizes, she who is doomed to dies, that is, Judaeo-Christian civilization. But if Europe is to see the light of a more or less distant future, she will have a meaning, historically, only if she is, as Friedrich Nietzsche desired her, sustained and organized by a new Myth, something radically foreign to everything contemporary.

We believe that this new Myth is already here, that it has already appeared. Of this there are signs, and signs behind the signs. At its origin, a Myth is always extremely fragile. Its life depends upon the few handfuls of men who already tell it. In a study of what I call European

---

2 Today, both tendencies have dissolved into liberal, Western society. — Ed.

music from Johann Sebastian Bach to Richard Wagner, I tried to show how this New Myth and the historical conscience that sustains it were born, and to show by which path this New Myth has reached the present.[3]

If it still lives, it can only survive through the total fidelity of those who sustained it in its recent past.

Of course, it has not yet told all it has to tell. Perhaps it has only stammered.

Myth, for as long as it lives, is always being told.

---

3   See *Wagner, Nietzsche et le mythe surhumaniste*, also published in the Agora series (Paris: Institut Iliade–La Nouvelle Librairie, 2022). — Ed.

II

ROOTS

This article appeared over the signature 'N. E.' in the usual 'Itinéraires' rubric that introduced the special issue of *Nouvelle École*, 'Georges Dumézil et les études into-européennes' ('Georges Dumézil and Indo-European Studies'), no. 21–2 (winter 1972–3). The paternity of the text, whose content, in truth, leaves little room for doubt, has been confirmed by Pierluigi Locchi. Here we find densely summarized the reasons the 'Indo-European fact' is so central to our present and, above all, to our future. The discoveries of archaeology, anthropology and especially linguistics, recently elaborated by Dumézil's comparative mythology, are here combined with searingly relevant reflections on the 'biopolitical' revolution and the advent of the 'third man,' which today confront us with a transition of such a critical height as to have comparable precedents only in mankind's origination or in the Neolithic Revolution.

1

Indo-European Identity and the Modern World

'INDO-EUROPEAN' IS, as we know, the term conventionally indicating a language spoken at the beginning of the Neolithic whose 'discovery,' by means of a linguistics based upon a science (in the modern sense of the term), dates to the first decades of the nineteenth century. Since every language requires users, the discovery of an Indo-European *language* (namely, Indo-European) was also the discovery of a group of *speakers* (the Indo-Europeans), that is, a *people* and a *civilization*, to the recovery of whose dimensions and the study of whose characteristics Georges Dumézil and many others have dedicated their efforts.

Today we know with certainty what the men of the late eighteenth century did not: that in a distant past there existed an 'Indo-European people,' and that this people's language was the direct ancestor of a great many languages spoken in Antiquity and in our own time, specifically the Neo-Latin, Germanic, Celtic, Baltic, Hellenic, Slavic and Indo-Aryan languages. We also *know*, and with no less certainty, that the Indo-European inheritance *formed* the civilizations that gave birth to 'European civilization,' and that this inheritance still carries a certain 'world-perception' (*Weltsicht*), if only in *linguistic fact*, and whose substance is in tatters, these days, but which remains active as the constructive force of representation which structures our thought.

One sees the primary reason for our interest in the *res indo-europeana* at once. In a Europe called, by the exigencies of an increasingly *global* world, to transform its ancient civilizational unity into a new political unity, we all, or almost all, speak a Neo-Indo-European language, and are therefore all indebted to a single perception, beyond the millennia of *history*, which shapes our mentality and our destiny. In the closing pages of his work on linguistic terminology, *Einführung in die linguistische Terminologie* (Munich: Nymphenburger Verlagshandlung, 1971), Hans J. Vermeer writes: 'It is clear that the dichotomy [between verb and noun] made by historical Indo-European languages has made its mark on the Western world-vision, simply by structuring every individual's *lexicon* in advance. But this world-vision is a theory, and only one among many possibilities.'

It has become fashionable to question the foundations of this *Weltsicht*, this *theory in the form of a world-view*, innate to Neo-Indo-European languages, thus, naturally, opposed to the 'theories' of other languages. It is just as fashionable to answer this question in the negative. For example, European languages are criticized for their *capacity for abstraction*. Now, if this will and capacity to abstract was first expressed in undisciplined divagations, it was also the *conditio sine qua non* of all scientific thought and practice. Science, and scientific progress, are more or less exclusively indebted to the Western *mentality* and to those *historically*-oriented 'hot societies' which Claude Lévi-Strauss and others would have relapse into the cold, green paradise of the Bororós. Of course, the Indo-European inheritance appears to be a *limitation*: the world-perception it conveys is only *one* among thousands upon thousands of possibilities. But the same goes for any world-perception. And, in a world in which the principle of individuation is the condition of existence, and every existence is owed to a limiting decision, this inheritance is the only one, to our eyes, that is still *open* to the future.

Furthermore, and beyond all rational considerations, we feel ourselves to have the right to freely *decide* upon the Indo-European inheritance and the destiny bound up with it in an act of fidelity which — let us not deny it — is nobody's business but our own. Martin Luther said: 'Here I stand. I can do no other.' Living in an age that encompasses the moment Luther proclaimed his revolt, we believe we *know* we can be who we are because we will it, and because we can do no other.

※

If it is true, as we believe, that man can only be *understood as such* within his own peculiar framework, that is, the *historical framework*, then one cannot help but take an interest in the Indo-European fact, since this fact is a *past* which, we see *at once*, is written into our *present*. But there are other reasons for our interest. Our interest is polarized, at one level, by the *scientific method* that allowed nascent linguistics to 'discover' the Indo-Europeans and, at another level, by the *object* of that discovery, by the *Indo-European origins* that provide a unique example of the *regeneration of history* which *our* age seems to demand once more.

The discovery of the Indo-European language by means of the comparative method is, from the strictly scientific perspective, no less crucial a revolution for the human sciences than the discoveries of the elementary particles and the discrete nature of energy were for physics.

The contemporary vogue for *synchronic* linguistics, taken by many to be the 'model' of the human sciences (perhaps because it so often collapses into a complex discourse upon its own vacuity...), distracts us from the fact that this sort of linguistics is, historically speaking, a mere derivative of *diachronic* linguistics, and that it started, with Saussure, from a reflection upon the (implicit and explicit) axioms and procedures of diachronic linguistics. To take just one example, structuralist linguistics, 'mother' of all our various contemporary structuralisms, simply states what early-nineteenth-century linguists took for granted, while assuming the airs of its discoverers: to wit, that every language is *structured* and constitutes a *system*. If Bopp, Rask and

Grimm were able to 'reconstruct' the Indo-European language at the beginning of the nineteenth century, that was because they based their method on the comparison of (phonetic and morphological) *systems*, as, moreover, the titles of some of their works make clear.

Therefore, contemporary synchronic linguistics cannot justify its reflections *by itself*. It can only fine-tune the linguistic *instrument* necessary for diachronic investigations which draw upon historical fact, the human fact *par excellence*. Synchronic linguistics folds in upon itself and leads unavoidably to what they call *reductionism*, the illegitimate attempt to reduce the human, first to the zoological, then to the biological, before 'reabsorbing' it, as Lévi-Strauss would say, into the 'physicochemical.'

Diachronic linguistics, meanwhile, has always and unhesitatingly stepped up to serve the true human science, which is *history*. Better still, it has singlehandedly overturned our conception of history and revealed the characteristics of *historical spacetime* distinct from macrophysical, microphysical and biological spacetimes. The first to break the barrier of *direct testimony*, on which all historical study had till then been based, it was able to recover an entirely forgotten past, pushing *past the origin* written statement and into the 'silent millennia' which had, till then, been *thought* historically *void*, and *compressed* by the imagination into a sort of single moment of indefinite, *immobile* duration. Thanks to diachronic linguistics (and parallel developments in archaeology and anthropology), and in a flash, a historical period ('ultrahistory,' in Dumézil's terms) which we had only allotted seven or eight thousand years' 'duration,' attained a new *dimension* of tremendous depth which we have hardly begun to explore.

Finally, diachronic linguistics has one peculiar (and essential) feature: it seeks, and finds, testimonies to the *past* not — as an archaeologist or palaeontologist would, for example — in a *fossil* that only geological happenstance has preserved for us, but in a *contemporary fact*, to wit, modern man and the language he speaks. Therefore, the historical past is implicit, not as an earlier moment *forever lost*, but as a dimension of the historical age, in any moment of our present — and of our future.

But we must emphasize (and never forget) that this *past recovered from the present* only appears by means of a *new* perspective peculiar to a definite historical period, and to this period alone. Before (or rather *outside*) this period, *no such past existed*; and in the language proper to the bio-macrophysical perspective, it might even be said *no longer to exist*. Before the development of diachronic linguistics, the Indo-Europeans were *never* part of *history*, which knew nothing of them (much like some 'academic' history even today). They did not 'exist.' This need not keep us from calling fossils and relics of a bio-macrophysical sort 'Indo-European,' which is quite natural given that *historicity* is founded upon *human biology*. Nevertheless, we are aware that the obsolete present which such relics attest never belonged to an *Indo-European historical entity*. No people has ever called itself 'Indo-European,' or has understood that identity as we understand it today. Again, this is no surprise: for a historical fact becomes *real* only in human consciousness. The *Indo-European fact* only enters history and becomes *historically active* once 'discovered,' that is, at the moment a human consciousness, bound to a peculiar 'epochal' perspective — our own consciousness and perspective — *reconstructs* it *as the past of its own present*.

So, it is no exaggeration to say that the real *Indo-European fact* is such only *in* and *through us*. It is our projection of ourselves onto the past, but, at the same time, the reinvented *myth* through which we project ourselves onto the future. If we were Marxists, we might say that the Indo-European fact is, in its 'mythic substance,' the *theory* of our *practice*. And it is on this account that we may speak of the Indo-European inheritance as a 'free decision' which is the past we give ourselves from among a thousand other possibilities.

ஃ

It is still said that history was born in Sumer. But that is not true. It is *no longer* true. But nor did history begin with the Cro-Magnon and his cave-paintings, which are, for those 'modern' historians who are determined to recognize historicity and 'humanity' only in the human type with which the Neolithic Revolution originated (*Homo sapiens sapiens*), ersatz equivalents of Sumer and writing. Here, too, since the early nineteenth century, advances in palaeoanthropology have allowed us to broaden our *historical perspective*. For us, history begins (and begins anew) wherever the prehuman *becomes human* by uniting gesture and word as attested by the invention and employment of the tool, the discovery of fire, *etc.*

It was certainly not by chance that the discoveries of palaeoanthropology and the *Indo-European fact* coincided with the moment a sense of *Zeit-Umbruch*, the 'rupture' of historical time, seized the minds of Europe, some reading it as the announcement of the *end of history*, the decisive eschatological event that would allow man to quit this 'vale of tears,' and others, on the contrary, as the sign of a *regeneration of history* and a new beginning. The discovery of the history, beyond the wall of text, of 'Classical' civilizations' Indo-European roots *responds* to the needs of a time of crisis unable to imagine or to will a *historical future* (except from a purely eschatological perspective) without first recovering a *new past* and, with it, a new opportunity for an *authentic decision*.

The nineteenth century began during a time of transition, a period marked by the radical transformation of our *Umwelt*, our environment. Now, from the old historical perspective, the radical transition *par excellence* was the abrupt transition from the *natural* (prehuman) to the *historical* (human). It was therefore imagined, by mere analogy, that the crisis of modernity, inasmuch as it represented a radical transition, must mean the *return from the historical to the natural*. From this perspective, man's evolution is believed to take a round trip, outward and homeward, between an *alpha* and an *omega*; between a terrestrial and a celestial paradise; between the primitive communism of the prehuman *acted upon* by nature and the post-historical communism of man 'returned' to nature with the abolition of all 'exploitation' and 'repression of instinct.' Of course, from our own perspective, a return to nature (an 'end of history') is always possible; but this return (this 'end') is not *logically necessary*. It does not express some mysterious superhuman will, nor any predetermination of man's destiny. Another possibility suggests itself: the regeneration of history, the advent of the 'third man,' a new human *adventure*. And the decision between these two possibilities falls to man, and to him alone.

◊

So far, there have been two men. One made himself man. He 'domesticated' himself by means of *science*, which, once upon a time, was 'magic.' The other asserted himself as man *tout court*, denying the 'humanity' of the first. His history is inextricable from the history of his 'domestication' of *living matter*. Today, man reaches another milestone, 'domesticating' *energy-matter*. Consequently, his environment is again radically transformed. But at the same time, he refuses to become fully conscious of the implications of this transformation. He refuses to *transform himself*. Therefore, he experiences the transformations of the modern world as a sort of *external* constriction that overcomes and alienates him. Modern mankind is a sorcerer's apprentice. 'I never asked for this,' he complains. He harps complacently on his 'restlessness,' his 'anguish,' *etc*. The nuclear threat, pollution, demographic explosion, the rise of the machine, the 'dehumanization' of society, the race for economic growth: it all becomes a pretext for halting this evolution that 'goes too fast,' that 'has no meaning.' Everything becomes an excuse to escape into the dream of 'arresting progress.'

In such a situation, the *Indo-European fact* acquires an exemplary value. Our Indo-European origins date, in fact, to another age of radical transformation: the *transition* represented by the *Neolithic Revolution*. The religion, ideology and social organization of Indo-European groups, excellently researched by Dumézil, comes in *response* (to be the only decent response, from our point of view) to the exigencies of that Revolution, which were no less anguishing than those we undergo today. Fortified by this 'response,' societies founded by the Indo-Europeans, inheriting their *attitude* to life, were able to *take responsibility* for the world of the 'second man.' They pushed the dynamic governing the relations between the 'domesticators' of living matter and the 'domesticated' matter itself to its conclusion, clearing the way to a *new future* thanks to new techniques for the 'domestication' of energy-matter.

Despite its urgent relevance, and the sense that we are only beginning to get to know its creators, the Indo-European inheritance seems to have been 'forgotten,' sometimes *deliberately* forgotten, and often despised. No surprise there. The histories of Rome, Greece or Germany were *acceptable* from the old perspective, insofar as their 'events' were understood to prefigure and prepare the advent of Christianity and the egalitarian *oecumene*. The moment we saw *whence* these historical currents came and whither they might go, it seemed 'preferable,' to some, to *suppress* them and to blur their outlines. Contemporary European scholarship no longer wants to learn Greek of Latin.

The key to this erasure, this *wilful* forgetfulness, is the eschatological character and will of contemporary societies. Western societies, the inheritors of Indo-European society, are, says Lévi-Strauss, 'hot societies,' essentially dynamic, always in motion, animated by a 'deadly' *will to history*. So, they must disappear — or at least 'cool off.'

The only *positive* response to the problems and challenges of our time is to adopt an *attitude* that reproduces *by adapting and reinventing* the attitude of the Indo-Europeans who confronted the Neolithic Revolution. Therefore, our reflections begin with the *fact of our Indo-European origins*, with that past recovered from our present, which allows is to discern the *questions* our age poses us and the *responses* we might give.

᛫

The 'example' of our Indo-European origins is only surprising on first glance. Examined up close, we see that the *trifunctional society* reconstructed by Georges Dumézil organizes only *two castes* or social groups. The first, dominant caste assumes the sovereign and martial functions, following an initial separation into 'age-classes.' The second assumes the economic function. Now, thanks to Georges Dumézil's work, we now know that this *trifunctional society* was reflected in (and took its ideal model from) the *society of the gods*, whose *myths* reveal society's genesis.

These myths indicate that trifunctional society is formed by the superimposition of the first caste over the second, of the *magician* over the *religious man*, of predator over producer. The myths of the Æsir and Vanir, not unlike those of the Latins and Sabines already examined in these pages,[1] reveal the characters of these two social groups or families of gods. The first, the 'predator-gods,' continuators of the 'first man' as *self-domesticator*, impose themselves through the *binding* magic of their chief, Óðinn–Wotan. The second, the 'producer-gods,' continuators of the 'first man' as *self-domesticated*, are compelled (and agree) to submit, despite the power given them by the 'bounty' symbolized by Gullvieg's gold.

This 'social–divine' dichotomy derives from a particular *Weltsicht*, from a worldview prominently reflected in the Indo-European *linguistic* structure with its clean *separation of subject from object* (we see an 'imperialism' of subject over object comparable to the 'imperialism' of the *subject-gods* of the first group over the *object-gods* of the second). Moreover, this *synchronic* organization, which preserves the past in the present, is mirrored by a *diachronic* organization. For the Æsir, as the *first* gods, are the sons or grandsons of 'Cosmic Man' who, myth tells us, was present at the origin of the world (or, more precisely, of the *new world*).

---

1 See the next chapter, 'The Indo-European Cosmogonic Myth: Reconstruction and Relevance.' — Ed.

Here, vast fields of research and reflection open out. We need not labour the subject. But it already seems possible to identify some outlines of this Indo-European world-vision, which is, let us repeat, a *historical* vision above all.

The 'first man,' an *undivided Zwitter*, uniting all antinomies, all opposites in himself, *created himself through self-domestication*. He was both the subject and object of domesticating 'magic.' The 'second man' appears (along with the *new world*) once the 'first man' (Purusha, Ymir, Cosmic Man, *etc.*, in Indo-European myth) subdivides himself and *objectifies* himself in two *social* types: first, *subject-man*, who continues to work his 'magic' upon himself ('self-control')[2] while also turning it upon the other type, *object-man*, upon whom domesticating magic is worked *from without* (and whose *limits* are set by someone other than himself), and who, freed by this 'religious' bond from the need to domesticate himself, can dedicate himself fully to the 'domestication of nature,' that is, to the *production of goods*. The coexistence of these social types within a harmonious society is ensured by *synoecism* (a term suggested by Dumézil), that is, by contractual compromise following a 'war of foundation.' Note, moreover, that the Indo-European sovereign god is always both a *terrible* god, imposing 'magical' constraints, and a *beneficent* god, the guarantor of 'contracts.' From the Indo-European origins onwards, we find a clear conception of the 'social contract' which was surely most completely expressed by the Romans.[3]

Therefore, from the Indo-European example, we can deduce the *primacy* of true creative activity, that is, of *subjectivity with respect to oneself*. It cannot truly be said that the 'second man' is a progression

---

2 English in the original — Tr.

3 In Roman history, we find one extremely telling example. This is the 'historical' myth of the secession of the plebs, who, in 494 BC, for want of political and civil equality, 'withdrew' to Mons Sacer to found another city there. The crisis was resolved in 493 with the intervention of Menenius Agrippa (Consul in 503) who facilitated concord by telling the plebeians the transparent apologia for the *members and the stomach*. This apologia outlines the Indo-European conception of the 'social contract' in a striking way.

beyond the 'first.' He simply represents to a *rupture* realized objectively in primitive, unitary (*undivided*) society.

Nevertheless, the *separation* of types inevitably entails, like a reflex, the need to reconstitute man's *uni-totality* at the level, not of the individual, but of the *social ensemble*. Whence the compromise and the 'contract': from now on, man can only *realize himself* socially, within a *community*.

Indo-European society was therefore a 'hot society' characterized by its consciousness of (or at least an *instinct* for) its own historicity. Thus, at every moment, it bore its past, present and future within itself, *indissolubly bound*. As we have already observed, this co-actuality of past, present and future is asserted implicitly *in* and *by means of* the method of diachronic linguistics. Everything is connected. The *method* of a science is always imposed by its very *object*, just as a 'scientific object' is discovered, revealed and defined only through the method that fits it.

&

Therefore, we *project* the Indo-European inheritance we uncover and cultivate within ourselves onto history doubly, both as the re-presentation of the past, and as the 'imagination' of the future. In its very broadest sense, the term 'Indo-European' applies to everything that *pleases us* in the glorious spectacle of a future already lived by generations past; everything opposed to everything we dislike, to everything that leaves us cold. But the study and 'cult' of this past which *we have chosen* and which *has chosen us* are only one aspect, the *theoretical* aspect, of a *manifestation of will*. The other, *practical* aspect consists in the resistance against the retreat from, the renunciation, the *reduction* (the arrest) of history, and in accepting (and even *willing*) 'all that is great and terrible in man.' That is, at the present moment, the outline of a *new* world, a new historical and tragic destiny.

Therefore, when we speak of the Indo-European tradition, or when we shed new light on the overgrown tracks of the myth, religion, ideology and history of the peoples we recognize as our ancestors, we are not just looking backwards. On the contrary. Like Janus Bifrons, we project upon the future. We set milestones along our way and sketch the models of the men and things we strive to create within and beyond ourselves.

This article, which was inaccessible for a long while — it appeared in *Nouvelle École*, no. 19 (July–August 1972) — is an essential key to understanding the basic outlines of Giorgio Locchi's thinking, casting highly original light on the nature, origins and significance of the blatant opposition between pagan, polytheist culture and the biblical world. This opposition is of course taken as given by those who do not subscribe to the universalist and fundamentally 'American' vision of the 'transcendental unity of all religions' — to which modern intellectuals are especially susceptible, who, though they speak a great deal about 'tradition,' tend to ignore in their works the available data on traditions themselves in favour of insupportable fantastical, philological and anthropological reconstructions. The present text also deserves to stand where the real traditions that have driven our history are born, aiding ultimately the overcoming of this vaguely metaphysical traditionalist night in which all cats are as black as each other. The true dichotomy is no longer between a purported past 'golden age' and the later rise of the 'revolution,' 'progress' or 'materialism,' but between coexisting historical tendencies, whose religious or secularized form ultimately proves entirely secondary to the world-visions they concretely advance.

2

The Indo-European Cosmogonic Myth: Reconstruction and Relevance

To Mr. Georges Dumézil

'Ich sagte dir, ich muss hier warten, bis sie mich rufen.'[1]

Orestes in *Elektra*, Hugo von Hofmannsthal

THE ANCIENT Indian *Rig Veda* and the Germanic *Edda* present two great *cosmogonic* myths (that is, relating the creation of the world) which agree to such an extent that one might quite rightly discern in them two derivatives of one *common Indo-European myth*. Perhaps some echoes of this myth may be found among the Greeks. Rome, as we shall see, never forgot the 'protagonist' of this *sacred drama* in which our Indo-European ancestors saw the *beginning of the world*. But the drama itself has only reached us in its entirety via Germanic and Indo-Aryan intermediaries, who thereby show themselves to have the 'longest memory,' at least by the time they entered 'written history.'

With his admirable work on *trifunctional ideology*, Mr. Georges Dumézil has brought a fundamental and absolutely *original* aspect of the Indo-European religion and *Weltanschauung* to light. No less essential, no less *original*, is the belief in the *primacy of man* (and of the human) which the Indo-European cosmogonic myth as 'preserved' by

---

[1] 'I told you—I must wait here till they call me.'—Tr.

the *Rig Veda* and *Edda* attests. For the Indo-European, *man is present at the origin of the universe*. From him all things — gods, nature, life-forms and, ultimately, himself — proceed as historical being. However, as Mrs. Anne-Marie Esnoul remarks, 'this beginning is only a relative beginning. It is an eternal principle which creates the world but, after a given period, destroys it' (*La naissance du monde*, Seuil, 1959). For the Indo-Europeans, man is not only present at the origin of the universe. He *is* the origin of this universe in which mankind lives and *becomes*. For, in the beginning, says the myth, was *Cosmic Man*: Purusha in the *Rig Veda*; Ymir in the *Edda*; Mannus, as Tacitus mentions, among the continental Germans (Manu was also known to the Indians as the ancestor of mankind).

Cosmic Man: Ymir, Purusha

In the tenth book of the *Rig Veda*, the tale of the beginning of the world begins as follows:

> A thousand heads hath Purusha, a thousand eyes, a thousand feet.
>
> On every side pervading earth he fills a space ten fingers wide.
>
> This Purusha is all that yet hath been and all that is to be;
>
> The Lord of Immortality which waxes greater still by food.
>
> [...]
>
> All creatures are one-fourth of him, three-fourths eternal life in heaven.[2]

Purusha is therefore the One Thing through whom the universe begins. He is formed and rises from the 'chaotic waters,' from the 'unfathomed depth of water,' from 'indiscriminated chaos' — apparently all that remains of the previous universe.[3]

In the *Edda*, the 'Völuspa' tells us:

---

2   10.90, *The Hymns of the Rigveda*, tr. R. T. H. Griffiths (Benares: Lazarus, 1895), pp. 517-8. — Tr.

3   10.129, ibid., p. 575. — Tr.

> Of old was the age when Ymir lived;
>
> Sea nor cool waves nor sand there were;
>
> Earth had not been, nor heaven above,
>
> But a yawning gap, and grass nowhere.[4]

The initial organization of the world comes from Ymir, also the *undivided* One. 'Grímnismál' explains:

> Out of Ymir's flesh was fashioned the earth,
>
> And the ocean out of his blood;
>
> Of his bones the hills, of his hair the trees,
>
> Of his skull the heavens high.[5]

The same happens in the *Rig Veda*:

> The Moon was gendered from his mind, and from his eye the Sun had birth;
>
> Indra and Agni from his mouth were born, and Vāyu from his breath.
>
> Forth from his navel came mid-air; the sky was fashioned from his head;
>
> Earth from his feet, and from his ear the regions. Thus they formed the worlds.[6]

Purusha is therefore Prajāpati, 'father of all creatures.' For the gods themselves represent only 'one-fourth' of Cosmic Man. And he alone restores mankind in the end. As we read in the *Rig Veda*: 'With three-fourths Purusha went up: one-fourth of him again was here.'[7]

As the *undivided* One, Cosmic Man is a *Zwitter*, a *Zwitterwesen*, an asexual being or, more precisely, potentially *androgyne*. He reconciles the two sexes, still intermingled, in himself. Moreover, Indian theology teaches that 'male' and 'female,' along with all '*complementary*

---

4 *The Poetic Edda*, tr. Henry Adam Bellows (New York: ASF, 1923), p. 4. — Tr.
5 Ibid., p. 100. — Tr.
6 10.90, Griffiths, op. cit., p. 519. — Tr.
7 Ibid., p. 518. — Tr.

opposites,' issue from the 'division of Purusha.' Ymir, meanwhile, sleeps in the ice of the Yawning Abyss (Ginnungagap) that separates north from south, while two giants, one male, one female, form as excrescences under his armpits. And similarly, from him, or from the ice that he fertilizes, the first human couple, Borr and Bestla, is born, to become the progenitors of the first Æsir (or sovereign deities), Wotan (Óðinn), Vili and Ve.

When interpreting these great cosmogonic myths, one must never forget that, for the Indo-European mentality, *reciprocal generation* is a totally normal process. 'Logical opposites' are always complementary and perfectly equivalent. They *posit* one another mutually. Thus, *man* in the singular gives birth to the gods (or draws them from himself) while the gods, in turn, give birth to *men* in the plural (or breathe the spirit of life into them). According to the *Edda* ('Völuspá'):

> Then from the throng did three come forth,
>
> From the home of the gods, the mighty and gracious;
>
> Two without fate on the land they found,
>
> Ask and Embla, empty of might.
>
> Soul they had not, sense they had not,
>
> Heat nor motion, nor goodly hue;
>
> Soul gave Othin, sense gave Hönir,
>
> Heat gave Lothur and goodly hue.[8]

Clearly, in this tale, the first three Æsir play the parts of the first 'civilizing heroes.' Ask (that is, the ash-tree) and Embla (that is, the elm) represent mankind still 'immersed in *nature*,' entirely subject to his species, recalling the bygone age of Borr. Moreover, by imagining oneself back at the *time* of the Indo-European society governed by trifunctional organization, one will see how each class assumes one of the three functions, appearing as the descendants of the god Heimdall

---

8   Bellows, op. cit., p. 8. — Tr.

and of three human women. 'Rígsmál' relates how Heimdall, assuming the appearance of Ríg, begets Thræll, ancestor of slaves, upon *Ahne* ('ancestor'), *Karl*, ancestor of peasants, upon *Emma* ('wetnurse'), and Jarl, ancestor of nobles, upon 'Mother.'[9] On the other hand, in the *Rig Veda*, the lineages of the social classes flow directly from the primordial Cosmic Man:

> The Brahman was his mouth, of both his arms was the Rājanya made.
>
> His thighs became the Vaishya, from his feet the Shūdra was produced.[10]

Janus, Ambiguous God

As this apportioning of classes suffices to show, the *Rig Veda*'s 'version' seems to be more faithful to the original Indo-European story. The Germanic version may still derive from a very ancient source. Heimdall is a highly mysterious figure. Mr. Dumézil has admirably explained the peculiar essence of this god, who is the Germanic correlate of the Roman Janus and the Indian Vāyu. Chronologically, Heimdall is first of the Æsir, the oldest of the gods. He is also an *all-seeing god*: 'He hears the grass push through the earth, the wool grow on the sheep's back. Nothing escapes his piercing gaze.'[11] Therefore, he stands watch over Asgard, the 'home of the Æsir.' From him came the beginning; from him shall come the end, *Ragnarøkkr* (or 'twilight of the gods'), which he announces by sounding a horn. So, Heimdall unites in himself all the characteristics of the 'Supreme Being,' the object of a more ancient worship which Raffaele Pettazzoni attributes to *primitive humanity* (that is, to humans at the end of the Mesolithic), and also corresponds to the 'forgotten god,' of whom Mircea Eliade speaks, the vague reminiscence by 'evolved' religions of a past conception of divinity. We may therefore take Heimdall to be the *projection* of the 'Supreme Being'

---

9   Cf. ibid., p. 201, ff. — Tr.
10 Griffith, op. cit., p. 519. — Tr.
11 Snorri Sturlusson, *Gylfaginning*, 27.

of the *Indo-Europeans' ancestors* into the society of 'new gods,' just as Ymir *continues* it at the level of cosmogony as a 'universal principle.'[12] This reading throws new light on the 'problem of *Janus*,' another mysterious deity who, as we said, is the Roman correspondent of the Germanic Heimdall. Much debate has been had over the etymology of the name 'Janus.' For a long time, it seemed to have been agreed that it derived from the Indo-European root *ya, related to ideas of 'passing' or 'going.' But this is not very convincing; and one wonders why 'Janus' ought not rather to be traced to the roots **yeu(m)* or **yeu(n)* (whence Latin *iungo, iungere* and French *joug, joindre, conjoint, conjugal*, etc.), related to ideas of 'uniting,' 'joining the separate' and therefore of 'pairing *opposites*' ('logical opposites'). This would explain the *ambiguous* character of this *deus bifrons* who is, like Ymir, a *Zwitter*.

Ancestor of the Ancient Latins

Moreover, we know that one of Janus' ancient appellations, whose significance had been forgotten by Augustus' time, was *Cerus Manus*, translated as 'benevolent creator' (from *ker, 'to make increase,' and the hypothetical *man, 'good'). One would rather say that *Manus* is simply an Indo-European 'fossil' preserved in Old Latin and tracing back to 'Mannus' and meaning 'man,' as in Germanic and ancient Indian. Moreover, Latin *immanis* does not mean 'bad' or 'evil' but rather 'prodigious,' 'out of bounds' (*inhuman*: beyond the bounds of the human). One sees, then, why Janus, who is (like Heimdall) god of the prima (of 'things chronologically prior'), was understood, as *Cerus Manus*, to be the ancestor of the tribes of Latium, just as Mannus was the ancestor of the Germanic tribes.

---

12   The *Rig Veda* expressly states that Purusha, the Indo-Aryan correlate of Ymir, has 'a thousand heads' and 'a thousand eyes' which shows that Cosmic Man is originally endowed with omnivoyance. For Pettazzoni, omnivoyance was one of the characteristics of the *primitive Supreme Being*.

The 'Dismemberment' of God

Vedic ritual, which revolved around the notion of *sacrifice*, takes the *dismemberment*, the 'division' of Cosmic Man (Purusha) as the prototype of sacrifice. Now, in 'speculative' texts, Purusha's sacrifice is presented in two forms: first, Purusha *sacrifices himself*, thereby making the 'imperishable sacrifice'; and second, the gods sacrifice Purusha and 'dismember' him. The question is whether the Indians were 'interpreting' or whether they were preserving an Indo-European tradition in all its purity. The latter seems more likely, if only because all myth, at its origin, is both the *story* of a rite and its *projection*. Moreover, this *double* image is found in the *Edda*. Purusha's 'dismemberment' is mirrored, albeit in a *desacralized* form, by Ymir's 'dismemberment' by the Æsir, sons of Borr. As for the other, *self-sacrificial* aspect of Cosmic Man's sacrifice, it suffices to refer to the 'Song of the Runes' ('Rúnatálsþáttr'), where Wotan declares:

> I ween that I hung on the windy tree,[13]
> Hung there for nights full nine;
> With the spear I was wounded, and offered I was
> To Othin, myself to myself,
> On the tree that none may ever know
> What root beneath it runs.[14]

Wotan–Óðinn, the sovereign god, is by no means Cosmic Man, and does not play that part among the society of gods.[15] But even if he is not at the origin of the universe, Wotan is at the origin of the universe's *new order*. It falls to him to inaugurate man's 'second age' (the properly *historical* age) with his sacrifice. Wotan–Óðinn sacrifices himself, not, like Purusha, to 'divide' and thus 'unleash' the opposites by which the universe is *shaped*, but to acquire the *knowledge* (the 'secret of the runes') which will allow him to organize or, more precisely, to

---

13   Yggdrasil, the world-tree.
14   Bellows, op. cit., p. 60. — Tr.
15   This part, as we have seen, is partially projected onto Heimdall.

reorganize the universe. In truth, this "refitting" of the original myth is no surprise. The Germanic *Weltanschauung* has always *emphasized* and *amplified* the Indo-Europeans' *historical imagination*, stressing the process of *becoming* in which past and future are *contained* in the present and are *transfigured*.

Implications of the Myth

The Indo-European cosmogonic myth never ceased to inspire and nourish ancient Indian imagination and speculation over the centuries. Perhaps its riches were never displayed with more splendour than in Kālidāsa's magnificent poem *Kumārasambhava*, in which Purusha is Brahmā, the divine personification of sacrifice.

> Praise be to You, O God in three forms,[16] You who were absolute unity before creation was complete, You who divided Yourself between the three gunas, from which You take Your names.[17] O never born, Your seed was not sterile when it was thrown into the watery wave! From You the Universe arose, which is lively and lifeless, and which lauds You as its origin in song. You have unleashed Your power in three forms. You alone are this world's creative principle and the cause, likewise, of all that is and shall pass away. From You, who divided Your own body in order to give birth, flow man and woman as parts of Yourself. They are called the Parents of creation, who go forth and multiply. If You, who separated day from night according to the measure of Your own time, if You sleep then all beings die; but if You life, they spring to life.
>
> With Your own self you know Your own being. You create yourself; but You lose Yourself in Your knowing Yourself in Your own self. You are Liquid; You are Solid; You are the Great and the Small, the Light and the Heavy, the Manifest and the occult. [...]
>
> You are called Prakriti;[18] but You are also called Purusha, who sees Prakriti in truth, but does not depend upon her. You are the father of fathers, the

---

16 The *Trimūrti*: Brahmā, Vishnu and Shiva.
17 Absolutely good Being; the Passion which obscures the spirit; and Ignorance.
18 Prakriti corresponds, in a way, to *natura naturans*.

god of gods. You are above the most high. You are the sacrificial offering, and likewise the presider over sacrifice. You are the sacrificial victim, but likewise the maker of the sacrifice. You are what we must know: the sage, the thinker, but likewise the highest object available to thought.

Kālidāsa's hymn is one of the summits of Indian 'poetic reflection' on the Vedic tradition. It beautifully teases out all the *implications* of the Indo-European cosmogonic myth, while bringing all its variations (successive or otherwise) on the original theme to unity. For example, the opposition between Purusha and Prakriti is very revealing, especially alongside the opposition between Purusha and the 'indiscriminated chaos,' or Ymir and the 'yawning abyss.' *Because he 'sees Prakriti in truth, but does not depend upon her,' Cosmic Man is at the origin of the universe.* Because the universe is merely an indistinct chaos, lacking any meaning or significance, from which only man's gaze and word can cause the multitude of things and beings, including man himself, to *arise*, realized at last. Purusha's sacrifice is, if you prefer, the *Apollonian moment* in which the *principium individuationis* is asserted, 'the cause of all that is and all that shall be' until the moment of the world's 'passing away,' that is, the *Dionysiac moment*, the end which is simultaneously the condition of a new beginning.

According to this *Weltanschauung*, the gods themselves are only 'one-fourth' of Cosmic Man. 'Superior Men,' in the Nietzschean sense, sustain them with the *transfiguring* memory of the first 'civilizing heroes,' those who led mankind from his 'past' state (that of Ask and Embla) and who *founded* the *human* society, the society of Indo-European man, by ordering it into three functions. These gods do not represent the Good. Nor do they represent Evil. They are at once Good and Evil. In this respect, they all present an ambiguous aspect (a *human* aspect), which explains why, as long as the *mythic imagination* governs their representation, they tend to come in pairs: Mitrā–Varuṇa, Jupiter–Dius Fidius, Óðinn–Ullr (Wōdanaz–Tīwaz), etc. For modern mankind, whom they *established as such*, these gods serve effectively as ancestors. Legislators, *inventors* of social traditions and, as such, ever-present, always active, they are nevertheless subject to *fatum* and doomed, very *humanly*, to an 'end.'

In conclusion, this is a matter of gods as *creatures* rather than creators; of *human* gods who nonetheless *order* the world and society; of the *ancestral* gods of 'modern' mankind; and ultimately, of gods 'as great in good as in evil,' who stand beyond these notions.

A Diametrically Opposite Direction

What we call the *Indo-European people* was in fact a society dating from the beginning of the Neolithic whose *myth* was constructed from the new *perspective* inaugurated by the 'Neolithic Revolution' by means of a reflection upon the beliefs of the foregoing period culminating in a *revolutionary* reformulation of the ancient *Weltanschauung*'s themes.

If, as Raffaele Pettazzoni, author of *L'omniscience de Dieu*, believes, 'primitive mankind,' that is, human groups at the end of the Mesolithic, believed in a Supreme Being (not to be confused with the monotheists' *single* God!), then the Indo-European cosmogonic myth is effectively the revolutionary reformulation of this belief (or, if you prefer, a *discourse* pushing the *language* and 'rationale' of the foregoing period to breaking-point and thus overcoming them). If this is so, we have every right to suppose that, for the Indo-Europeans' 'Mesolithic' ancestors, the 'Supreme Being' was nothing other than *man* himself or, more precisely, the 'cosmic projection' of man *as possessor of magical power*. And we see in the same glance that the Indo-Europeans' idea of a 'Supreme Being' was *not shared* by other human groups whom the Neolithic Revolution led to 'reflect' upon their ancient beliefs.

The classical East, for example, 'reflected' on, *imagined* and *reinterpreted* 'Mesolithic' beliefs in a direction diametrically *opposed* to the one the Indo-Europeans took. The Judaic Bible, a sort of *summa* synthesizing Eastern religious *Weltanschauungen*, stands at the antipode of the Indo-European 'vision.' But we do find there a 'reflection' on an *ancient theme*, with the 'Supreme Being' confronted, at the *beginning* of the world, by an earth 'without form, and void; and darkness was upon the face of the deep' (*Genesis*, 1.1). Of course, this 'yawning abyss' is immediately represented as the result of an *initial* creation by Elohim–Yahweh. Now, Yahweh does not create the universe through his own *division* and 'dismemberment.' He creates it *ex nihilo*, beginning with nothing. He is not the *coincidentia oppositorum*, the *undivided* One. He is not at once Being and Nonbeing. He is Being. 'I am that I *am.*'[19] Therefore, and since the created universe can never equal the creator-God, the world has no *essence* but only an existence, or, more precisely, some sort of 'lesser being,' an imperfection. While Indo-European polytheism is the complementary 'reverse' of what we might call their *monohumanism* (equivalent to a *panhumanism*), Judaic monotheism appears to be the *conclusion of a process of elimination*, the reduction of a *multiplicity* of nonhuman gods, personifying natural forces, to Elohim–Yahweh in his *solitude*,[20] in short, the result of *speculation* reducing the apparent plurality of things to a single principle, *which is not man, but matter and energy* ('nature').

Refusal

Because he is a *single*, unambiguous God, because he is not the point where 'logical opposites' coincide and resolve, Yahweh represents *absolute Good*. It is quite natural, then, that he should often prove cruel, merciless and jealous. Absolute Good cannot *not* be intransigent when it comes to Evil. What is less logical, though, is the biblical conception of *Evil*. Evil cannot come from absolute Good, and *cannot*, in fact, *exist at all* in a world created from *nothing* by a God of '*infinite* goodness.' But it does exist. This presents a serious problem. The Bible tries to solve it by making Evil the *accidental* consequence of the *revolt* of certain creatures, Lucifer first of all, against Yahweh's authority. So Evil manifests as the *refusal* of a *creature* to play the part Yahweh had assigned him. The power of Evil is formidable (since it derives from

---

19   *Exodus*, 3.14. — Tr.
20   Yahweh even admits that he is jealous of the 'other gods.' Is not the very term *Elohim* a plural (historic plural, not *pluralis maiestatis*)?

the rebellion of an angelic, thus privileged, creature); but beside the power of God, that is, Yahweh, it amounts to practically nothing. There can be no doubt, then, of the final *outcome* of Good's struggle against Evil. Every problem, every conflict is solved *in advance*. *History is pure deprivation*, the effect of impotent creatures' blindness.

Thus, from the very beginning, *history is void of meaning*. The first man (the first *mankind*) *sinned* by succumbing to one of Satan's suggestions. He thereby refused the part Yahweh had assigned him. He wanted to taste the forbidden fruit and *enter into history*.

With respect to 'contemporary' human society, Elohim–Yahweh, creator of the universe, plays a role perfectly *antithetical* to that of the Indo-Europeans' sovereign gods. He is not a 'civilizing hero' who *invents* a social tradition but the omnipotence who punishes Adam's 'sin,' that is, the *human* life he longed to taste, the *urban civilization* that developed from the Neolithic Revolution and to which *Genesis* implicitly refers. As Paul Chalus emphasizes (in *L'homme et la religion*), Yahweh has nothing but hatred for those 'bakers of bricks.' When he spies them building Babel and its famous tower, he cries: 'Now nothing will be restrained from them, which they have imagined to do. Go to, let us go down, and there confound their language, that they may not understand one another's speech' (*Genesis*, 11.6–7). Yahweh, Chalus adds, 'scatters them from there across the face of the earth; and they cease to build cities.' Well in advance of these events, Yahweh had refused the first-fruits that Cain, the *farmer*, offered him and only *regarded* Abel's pious offering. For Abel was not a pastoralist but a simple *nomad*, abandoning the hunt for the raid; he *continued the 'Mesolithic' tradition* in the midst of the new civilization to which the Neolithic Revolution had given birth, *forsaking* its mode of life. Later on, the mission of Abraham, a nomad who had abandoned the city (Ur), and his seed was to deny and to *internally withdraw* from every form of 'post-Neolithic' civilization whose existence sustains the memory of the 'revolt' against Yahweh.

Man is not the 'son' of the God of the Bible. He is a mere *creature*. Yahweh made him just as he made every other living being, much as a potter makes a vase. He made him 'in his own image and likeness,' to be his *superintendent* on earth, the guardian of Paradise. Adam, seduced by a demon, refuses the part his Lord bid him play. But man remains God's *serf*. 'Man's superiority over beast is nothing,' remarks Paul Chalus: 'for all is vanity.' 'All go unto one place; all are of the dust, and all turn to dust again' (*Ecclesiastes*).

Man, the Bible teaches, has nothing to do but perpetually to remember that he is dust, that every Job deserves the destiny that Yahweh's caprice has reserved for him, and that historical existence has no *meaning* beyond the one *implicit* in his *actively refusing* to recognize one. Israel's prophets, in their terrible voices, are always reminding Yahweh's elect of the imperious necessity of this refusal, just as the elect always see their misfortunes as fair punishment for some transgression (or mere forgetfulness) of Yahweh's supreme commandment.

The Creative 'Yes' and the 'No'

From its very beginning, 'Roman' Christianity, born from the 'Constantinian settlement,' was an attempt, in the midst of an 'ancient' world transformed by Rome into an *orbis politica*, to reach a compromise between the Indo-European *Weltanschauungen* and the Judaic religion which Jesus had striven to adapt to imperial Roman civilization.[21] Through the play of dogmatic *mystery*, the *single* God became one God 'in persons three.' He 'integrated' the old idea of the *Trimūrti*, of 'Trinity'; and its three 'persons' assumed the three functions of Indo-European society in an 'inverted' and spiritualized form. Though remaining *creator* and *sovereign*, Yahweh refuses to take on a *double aspect*. Evil remains Satan's exclusive domain. The *old name* the Bible had given him is substituted with a *new name*, *deus pater*, belonging to the 'eternal and divine father' revered by the Indo-Europeans. But

---

21   There is clearly no question of entering into this subject in detail here. We must stick to broad outlines.

Yahweh is only the *father* of his *second person*, the *son* who is sent to earth to play a role opposite to that of the 'civilizing hero'; the son who is *exiled* to *this* world only to return to the *other world*, and who only renders unto Caesar what is Caesar's because, in his eyes, what is Caesar's is of no value; the son whose *function* is not to 'make war' but to preach a *jealous* peace which can only benefit those men of 'goodwill,' those enemies of *this* world for whom eternity's only reward, the *grace* administered by the third 'person,' the Holy Ghost, is reserved.

Man, a creature, a *fabricated product*, is the serf of God, 'excrement' (*stercus*), as Augustine so nicely puts it. But *at the same time*, he is the *brother* of the incarnate son of Yahweh, making him an 'almost-son' of God, so long as he is wise enough to desire and deserve it, which depends entirely on the grace the creator administers according to unfathomable criteria. A day will therefore come when mankind will *definitively* divided (for all eternity) between the *blessed* and the *damned*. For there is a biblical Valhalla, Paradise; but it is now reserved for *antiheroes*. Hell is for the *rest*.

For centuries, this compromise shaped the history of what is called 'Western civilization.' For centuries, both 'pagan' and 'Eastern' man were able to see their *own* divinity in the *unus et trinus* God, according to their deep-set characters. This explains many notions, many confusions: first, the assimilation of Jesus, Siegfried and Barbarossa in Wagner's imagination, or the 'white God of the Gothic cathedral' so dear to Drieu La Rochelle; second, the Jesus of Ignatius of Loyola, the God of the worker-priest, and *Jesus Christ Superstar*.

Today, there can be no doubt that the Catholic–Constantinian 'settlement' was, in fact, no such thing, and that '*In hoc signo vinces*' was an April Fool whose aftershocks destabilized the Graeco-Romano-Germanic world. Till relatively recently, the Church of Rome and the other Christian *churches*, as organized secular power, seemed to stay faithful to the old compromise. But now they are attempting to *recognize* the authentic *essence* of Christianity. Yahweh the unrepresentable is now rescued, freed from the mask of the luminous and celestial Father-God, and proclaimed. Well in advance of the churches, though, a 'profane' (*demythicized* and desacralized) Christianity, that is, egalitarianism in all its guises, had recovered the biblical truth in its own way. The 'refusal of history' and explicit desire to 'exit history' (to return to *nature*); the *reductionist* tendency to 'reduce the human to the physicochemical,' determinist materialism, and the Marcusian condemnation of any art that betrays the 'truth' by integrating man into society; the egalitarian ideology that wants to *reduce mankind* to the antiheroic model, to the model of an elect hostile to all civilization, because they can see nothing in it but exploitation (Marx), repression (Freud) or pollution: all these have continued, and will continue, to *resuscitate* the immutable Yahwist vision (at the very moment a new technological *revolution* invites us to overcome the 'forms' imposed by the previous revolution), an 'eternal' vision if ever there was one, since it limits itself to the *endlessly repeated negation of every present pregnant with a future.*

A *yes* is not, cannot be 'eternal.' A *yes* is to the future: it *becomes*. In a history it never ceases to repropose by means of new *foundations*, this *yes* must always take on new forms and new contents. A *yes* is a *creation*, a work of art. A *no* only exists as a denial of this work's value. In a world where a clamour of voices, becoming countless, urge us to the contrary, the Indo-European cosmogonic myth reminds us that a *yes* is *always* possible; that a new Purusha–Ymir–Janus may yet stir himself from the 'indiscriminated chaos' where he slumbers; that he has perhaps *already* arisen; that he may *already* have sacrificed himself; that he may *already* have begotten Borr and Bestla; and that, soon enough, new Æsir, luminous gods, may stir with new life and, in *another* world *rising* from the chaotic *ruins* of the old, embark upon their eternal mission as 'civilizing heroes,' thus serenely assuming the splendid and tragic destiny of the man who *creates himself* and who, having begotten himself, accepts his own *end* as the condition of all historical adventure, of all life.

Here Locchi gives an exemplary lesson in the superhumanist reading of European culture's founding myths, meeting Lévi-Strauss's structural anthropology on its own ground: that is, the analysis of the meaning of a myth's very structure, aside from its manifest content or historical variants. At the time of the article's first publication in *Nouvelle École*, no. 17 (March–April 1972), structural anthropology was all the rage with the European intelligentsia and in publishing, no less than psychoanalysis or Marxism. Today, though debate on the subject has to an extent died down, the way of thinking associated with it has been entirely internalized by mass culture itself, even among those who want to oppose Western globalization. Which means that Locchi's contribution remains fundamental regarding many essential questions, even taking only its discussion on the 'nature–culture' relationship.

3

Lévi-Strauss and Structural Anthropology

WHETHER IN HIS first works[1] or in the series of 'Mythologiques,'[2] Mr. Claude Lévi-Strauss has only very rarely approached the problem of ancient Indo-European cultures. Whenever he has done so — always incidentally — his conclusions have generally owed their allure to what Mr. Edmund Leach has called 'an elaborate academic joke.'[3]

Perhaps the most extravagant of these Lévi-Straussian 'hoaxes' is the interpretation he gives the myth of Oedipus, an interpretation rapidly sketched, but which the author himself presents as an exemplum of his method.

Let us recall the broad outlines of this myth. Zeus, Father-God of the Hellenes, has abducted Europa, the daughter of king Agenor and the Aegean Telephassa. Her brothers, Phineus, Cadmus, Phoenix and Cilix, go to look for her. One of them, Cadmus, is accompanied by Telephassa. But she dies during the journey. Cadmus, unable to find his sister, goes to Delphi and consults the Oracle. The god instructs him to follow a cow bearing a lunar disc on its flanks, and to found the city of Thebes wherever the animal stops. The moment comes,

---

[1] *Les structures élémentaires de la parenté* (PUF, 1949); *Race et Histoire* (UNESCO, 1952); *Tristes tropiques* (Plon, 1955); *Anthropologie structural* (Plon, 1958). — Ed.

[2] *Le cru et le cuit* (Plon, 1964); *Du miel aux cendres* (Plon, 1966); *L'origine des manières de table* (Plon, 1968). — Ed.

[3] *Lévi-Strauss* (London: Fontana, 1996), p. 42. — Tr.

and, wishing to proceed with the foundation, Cadmus notices that the spring to which he goes to draw the water for sacrifice is guarded by a dragon, the son of Ares (Indo-European god of the warrior function). He succeeds in killing it, and, on the advice of a god, sows its teeth in the soil. From this strange seed springs a multitude of men, the Spartoi, who begin at once to kill one another. Then the survivors, numbering five, help the hero to build the city of Thebes. Having received the governorship over the Thebans from Zeus, Cadmus then makes peace with Ares, who gives him his own daughter, Harmonia, to wed.

One of Cadmus' descendants, Laius (from *laios*, 'left-sided), son of Labdacus (from *labdacos*, 'lame'), learns one day, through the intermediary of the Oracle at Delphi, that, if his wife Jocasta bears him a son, that son will kill him. So he throws Jocasta from his bed. The latter, vexed, manages to inebriate her husband, making him forget his resolution, and conceives a son, who receives the name Oedipus (that is, 'swollen foot,' from *oideō*, 'swell,' and *pous*, 'foot'). Fearing the vindication of the Oracle, Laius orders the infant to be put to death. But Oedipus, having been abandoned on a mountainside, feet bound, survives, and is welcomed by Polybus, king of Corinth. Come of age, he encounters Laius at a crossroads, argues with him, and, ignorant of their parental ties, kills him.

Creon, brother of Jocasta, then becomes regent of Thebes. A little later, the town is assailed by the Sphynx. Settled upon a rock, the monster poses questions to passers-by, and eats those who cannot answer. To rid himself of the Sphynx, Creon offers the hand of Jocasta in marriage to whoever can liberate the Thebans. Reaching the gates of Thebes, Oedipus succeeds in solving the riddle posed by the Sphynx, which throws itself down from its rock. So Oedipus weds Jocasta, not suspecting her to be his mother. From this incestuous union are born two sons, Eteocles and Polynices, and one daughter, Antigone. But one day, as a plague strikes the city, the truth is revealed to Oedipus by the seer Tiresias. So he gouges out his eyes and receives the gift of prophecy, while his mother kills herself. In one of the versions of the myth, Oedipus is banished from Thebes and wanders as a beggar, accompanied by his daughter Antigone. In another version, he continues to reign as king of the Thebans until the end of his days. At his death, Eteocles succeeds him with the support of Creon. But Eteocles soon faces the opposition of Polynices. The two brothers make war, and end by killing one another. Creon returns to power, and buries Antigone alive, who had dared, despite his sanction, to make a sepulchre for her brother Polynices, killed by Eteocles.

According to Lévi-Strauss, this myth expresses 'the inability, for a culture which holds the belief that mankind is autochthonous [...] to find a satisfactory transition between this theory and the knowledge that human beings are actually born from the union of man and woman.' This difficulty is supposed somehow to be 'insurmountable.' But, Lévi-Strauss adds,

> the Oedipus myth provides a kind of logical tool which relates the *original problem* — born from one or born from two? — to the derivative problem: born from different or born from same? By a correlation of this type, the *overrating of blood relations* is to the *underrating of blood relations* as the *attempt to escape autochthony* is to the *impossibility to succeed in it*.[4]

Let us begin by noting, the better to understand this jargon, that the *autochthony of man* is, with Lévi-Strauss, something of a dogma: every human myth implies the 'original belief' of human societies in their autochthonism. Let us also note that the word 'autochthonous' (normally meaning 'originating in the land one inhabits,' or, more rigorously, 'born from the earth,' 'one with the earth') here means 'born from one parent alone.'

As an attentive analyst, Lévi-Strauss has no trouble bringing the most *significant* elements of the myth to light. Unfortunately, once he begins to synthesise, to order the ensemble of these elements into a structure, his dogmatic (and, ultimately, ideological) prejudice comes

---

4   *Structural Anthopology*, tr. Claire Jacobson and Brooke Grundfest Schoepf (New York: Basic Books, 1963), p. 216. Locchi's emphases. — Tr.

very quickly to the fore, and leads him to genuine *nonsense*: the assertion of a 'Greek cosmology' based upon the 'autochthony of man,' from which the 'Oedipean problem' stems. He offers us the following table:

1. Overestimation of blood relations	2. Underestimation of blood relations	3. Negation of man's autochthony	4. Persistence of man's autochthony
Cadmus goes in search of Europa			
		Cadmus kills the dragon	
	Spartoi kill one another		Labdacus (Laius's father): lame
	Oedipus kills his father, Laius		Laius: left-sided
			Oedipus: 'swollen-footed'
		Oedipus defeats the Sphynx	
Oedipus marries his mother, Jocasta			
	Eteocles, son of Oedipus, kills his brother Polynices		
Antigone buries her brother Polynices, defying the ban of her maternal uncle, Creon			

One sees immediately that such an 'organisation' of the elements of the myth is already *interpretation*. Lévi-Strauss wishes to give us his personal message, and not that which the myth transmits. He therefore forces this latter in order to *inflect* it in the direction of a preconceived idea, and obliterates it in the same stroke. Taking care to *isolate* the myth of Oedipus (and its *variations*) from the entire context of Greek mythology, he treats what is in fact a *mytheme* as if it were a self-sufficient myth; he analyses a *theme* without regard for the *symphony*.

Such an interpretation is entirely foreign to the language of Hellenic myth, which, however, is transparent. Let us begin by taking what

Lévi-Strauss calls the 'overestimation of blood relation' (column 1) as an example. Here we find, in fact, a series of offences against the rules and taboos relating to *two concurrent* systems of kinship: the patrilineal and patrilocal system of the Indo-Europeans, and the matrilineal and matrilocal system of the aboriginal Mediterranean populations.[5]

If we are to believe Lévi-Strauss, Cadmus 'overvalued' the bonds of kinship that united him with his sister Europa: he went in search of her after her abduction, rather than leaving her to her fate. A funny way of seeing things! In fact, what is significant in this first 'episode' of the myth is the rape of the Mediterranean Europa (in one of the versions, her father Agenor, son of the Oceanid Libya, is the king of Phoenicia) by the Indo-European man newly arrived in Greece, represented here by Zeus. By taking a woman not his by right, Zeus violated the Mediterranean rule. Furthermore, having 'abducted' Europa, having taken her with him, he also contradicted the principle of *matrilocality*.[6]

In Oedipus' case, his union with Jocasta may appear at first to be a 'classic' incest. In reality, if one examines the context attentively, it amounts to a violation characterised by a rule stemming from matrilineal right, which stipulates that man be kin to his mother, and not to his father. Indeed, the incest uncovered, Jocasta punishes herself by killing herself. Oedipus, for his part, gouges out his eyes (an allegory for self-castration); but this blindness if overcompensated by the gift of prophecy. He is also guilty of having killed his father, therefore of having contravened the rule of absolute paternal right (and he know it). But, as we will see later on, Laius is a 'traitor' of the Indo-European tradition...

Perhaps Antigone's case is more revealing still, to the extent that the emphasis is placed upon the conflict between two conceptions, two

---

5 Greek societies, as is well-known, issue from a mixture of Mediterranean autochthones and immigrant Indo-Europeans.

6 This principle is illustrated by innumerable myths relating to the settlement of the Hellenes, which show heroes achieving kingship by wedding the daughter of a royal couple.

traditions, two irreconcilable jurisdictions. Indeed, the heroine incurs death for respecting the patriarchal rule, which requires that she bury her brother (replacing her father), despite the sanction pronounced *by her mother's brother*, Creon, representing matriarchal rule.

'Sons of Two'

When it comes to the 'underestimation of blood relation' (column 2), Lévi-Strauss inverts the facts of the matter once again. The Spartoi are, according to him, 'sons without a mother': therefore, in the jargon, *autochthones*, 'sons of one parent.' Maternal kinship is therefore undervalued here in the most absolute way. Now, this is entirely contrary to the truth. The Spartoi are the 'sons of the same and of the other' *par excellence*: that is, the product of the mixture of Indo-Europeans and Mediterraneans, the 'sons of *two* parents.' The dragon is the son of Ares, god of the second function among the Indo-Europeans (the warrior function), and consequently the grandsons of Zeus. The seeds (his teeth) fecundate the Mediterranean earth, which, as is well-known (including by Lévi-Strauss, who emphasises it on many occasions), represents the *mother par excellence*, and here symbolises the aboriginal populations with matrilineal societies. Furthermore, the meaning of the 'element' that the Spartoi represent is still more profound. It lays bare the very essence of the 'Greek problem.' If the Spartoi kill one another, it is precisely because they are 'sons of *two*,' the inheritors of two irreconcilable and antagonistic traditions, and because their society is the victim of permanent and extreme tension. The alliance between the survivors and Cadmus is a new symbiotic bond. Their participation in the building of Thebes, and their establishment in this city, lead one to think that the compromise is to the advantage, in fact if not by right, of the principle of matrilocality.

In column 3, the case of the dragon killed by Cadmus is effectively the *negation of man's autochthony*: for the dragon represents unilineal descent, the fact of being 'born of only one.' Here, the *nonsensicality* of Lévi-Strauss' expression is the consequence of the abstraction of his formula. In fact, what is here denied is not unilineal descent (*abstract*), but *uniquely* patrilineal descent (*concrete*). The dragon replaces Zeus, rapist of Europa. The fact that Cadmus fecundates the earth-mother with the teeth of the murdered dragon means that the order violated by the rape of Europa is substituted by a new order based upon 'compromise': bilineal descent (of father and mother), this compromise accommodating, let us recall, a 'preference' for matrilocality.

Lévi-Strauss places the murder of the Sphynx by Oedipus in column 3. Now, here again, the Sphynx does not represent autochthonism by any means, but rather its opposite: *bilineal descent*, with all the problems, all the *murderous* riddles that it involves for the members of the society that adopts it (and which *no longer understands* its own parentage; no longer knows how to answer its questions). Furthermore, according to legend, in order to punish Laius for his homosexual love of Chrysippus, the goddess Hera sent this monstrous being (*against nature*) to Thebes, of which all descriptions reflect its *hybrid character*: wings of a Harpy, tail of a dragon, body of a lion, face and breasts of a woman, *etc.*

Of the Left Hand

Lévi-Strauss is content to place Laius in column 4 ('persistence of man's autochthony') with his father Labdacus and his son Oedipus, having noted that these three persons, if one refers to the etymology of their names, have the fact that 'they walk clumsily' in common. They are, says, Lévi-Strauss, exceptional 'monsters.'[7] The reality is not so simple. We know that Labdacus is 'lame'; he only walks badly on one foot. Oedipus himself has two 'swollen feet.' As for 'left-sided' Laius, he walks *on the left-hand side*, which is the 'bad' side for the Indo-Europeans. Further, his being 'against nature' is illustrated by his homosexual relations with Chrysippus: he is a man who carries himself like a woman. Finally, he *does not wish* to have a son: when Oedipus is born,

---

7   Cf. ibid., p. 215. — Tr.

he orders him to be killed. The meaning of these repetitions seems evident. Laius wishes to establish, or to re-establish, the principle of matrilineal descent at Thebes, which favours daughters and excludes sons from inheritance. As for Oedipus, required to 'walk clumsily' (his feet were tied while he was abandoned on the mountainside), he kills Laius, not knowing him to be his father, and weds Jocasta, not knowing her to be his mother. The latter, once the incest is revealed, kills herself. Now, in the language of myth, to provoke suicide amounts to killing (as Lévi-Strauss is the first to recognise).

It can therefore be deduced that Oedipus *killed his mother by marrying her*. The whole story of the hero must then be interpreted as an attempt to put an end to an *ambiguous past* by restoring primacy to the Indo-European principles of patrilineality and patrilocality. By going to the end of his tragic destiny, Oedipus gouges out his eyes; but it is precisely at this instant that he *begins* to *see clearly*: the gift of prophecy overcompensates for blindness. Guided by Fate, he merely acts unconsciously. And that is why his attempt is abortive. Only an analogous but *fully conscious* action can cut the Gordian knot of intermixed traditions.

A Decisive Intervention

Such is the true meaning of the Oedipean *mytheme* in the context of Hellenic mythology. The myth of Oedipus has nothing to do with the risible and Byzantine problem of 'autochthonism,' of the unique *filiation* of man, as Lévi-Strauss has defined it. It concerns the *historical problem* that presented the Hellenes with two different, irreconcilable traditions. Beyond these variations, the myth establishes a *project*. It aims to force its listeners to solve the conflict by exclusively choosing the Indo-European patriarchal principle. *Greek tragedy*, which ensures the permanence of the myth's teaching, also unequivocally affirms as much.

Let us examine, for example, the famous *Oresteia* of Aeschylus. Agamemnon has killed his daughter Iphigenia, the sacrifice of whom was necessary to secure the victory over the city of Troy. He was 'permitted' this sacrifice: for the Indo-European father has the right of life and death over all the members of his *genos*. But his wife Clytemnestra, hearing the news at Argos, decides to avenge her. She kills Agamemnon with the aid of her lover Aegisthus, whom she makes king. Agamemnon leaves two children, Orestes and Electra. It is these who avenge their father by assassinating Clytemnestra seven years after her crime. For this crime, Orestes is hounded to madness by the Erinyes, guardians of Maternal Right. He ends up calling them to the tribunal at the Acropolis, where the god Apollo, representing Zeus, is his advocate. The Areopagus is also shared between partisans and adversaries of his acquittal. The ultimate decision falls to Athena, who tips the balance in Orestes' favour.

The way in which Athena makes her decision known is extremely significant. "With me it rests to give the casting vote," she says,

> And to Orestes I my suffrage pledge.
>
> For to no mother do I owe my birth;
>
> In all, save wedlock, I approve the male,
>
> And am, with all my soul, my father's child.
>
> Nor care I to avenge a woman's death
>
> Who slew her husband, guardian of the house.[8]

Thus the patrilineal and patriarchal principle triumphs utterly. Orestes, who *voluntarily* chose to be 'his father's son' *first of all*, and to repudiate his mother, there succeeds where Oedipus, who merely acted *unconsciously*, failed.

---

8   *Eumenides*, ll. 704–10, tr. Anna Swanwick, *The Dramas of Aeschylus* (London: Bell, 1886). — Tr.

Daughters Who 'Betray'

The parallel between Orestes and Oedipus is worth examining more deeply. Let us pause over the person of Athena, daughter of Zeus alone, goddess of the City, protectress of the State and symbol of Greek civilization. The justice she incarnates is a warrior justice. She always takes the side of her father. This is why she is always present in this tragic conflict between two antagonistic traditions. It is she who, through her 'equivalent,' Electra, exhorts Oedipus to avenge. But she is *also* the dragon, the 'son of a father alone' whom Cadmus kills. Now, it so happens that, by a subtle mythological irony, this goddess to whom the role of defending intransigently the Indo-European patriarchal principle is given is also, in a way, a 'converted goddess': a goddess originally belonging to the Mediterranean *pantheon* whom the Greeks adopted but radically *transformed*, making of her the *exact opposite* of a 'Mediterranean' goddess.

This 'conversion' of Athena must be reconciled with the mytheme of which Lévi-Strauss has spoken many times when he examines the 'variations' of the Oedipean myth, and which brings onstage the daughters who *betray their fathers to find their husbands*, but who, this treason accomplished (to the advantage of the suitor), are punished (killed or abandoned) by the same, rather than married. The classic example is that of Ariadne, who, besotted with Theseus, a Greek hero in Crete, betrays her father Minos (the episode of the Labyrinth and of the death of the Minotaur), and flees with her loves, before being abandoned by the same on the island of Naxos. From this mytheme, Lévi-Strauss deduces, *grosso modo*, that 'if societies are to continue to function, daughters must be unfaithful to their parents, while sons must destroy (replace) their fathers.' Stated in this way, the 'rule' becomes evidently absurd; and one might doubt the logic and good sense of the Hellenes. In fact, what this mytheme recommends to the Greek of the Indo-European tradition is quite simply to 'profit from circumstances' — that is, from feminine inclinations — in order to infiltrate matriarchal societies, while emphasising the overriding necessity to 'punish' those whose 'weaknesses' are exploited, so that the patrilineal and patriarchal principle is always preserved.

Couvade

Truth be told, it is quite difficult to see how Lévi-Strauss can have 'read' an incitement in the mytheme to 'murder (replace) the father' dear to his master *in ideologicis*, Sigmund Freud. Indeed, the 'betrayed' father is here the father of a foreigner, with whom the hero has no kinship. Still more, the 'betrayal' of the father by his daughter can be interpreted (the daughter replacing the mother) as a transposition of the 'sacred murder of the king,' which existed in certain matrilineal societies of an agricultural type (a ritual murder probably symbolizing the destruction of *paternal descent*, ensuring the validity of matrilineal descent). But among the Indo-Europeans, it is the 'mother's side' of decent that is destroyed; and this destruction takes pace in a rite derived from the *couvade*. In many primitive societies, the man mimics childbirth (the new-born is passed *through his legs*), a simulacrum signifying that the infant belongs to him *totally*. This *couvade* becomes allegorical among the Indo-Europeans: the father *engenders* the child and recognises it by taking it upon (that is, *between*) his '*genoux*.' In the Indo-European language, and in the languages derived from it, the man alone *engenders*; the woman 'bears,' 'brings into the world,' etc. Such terms as *genos* (family, in a broad sense), '*reconnaître*' (recognise), '*connaître*' (understand), 'engender,' '*genou*' (knee), all come from the same root: *$*gen$*, perhaps stemming from *$*eg$*, the paternal ego, the only to be genuinely recognised in social dialogue.

Science and Ideology

This brief excursion into the domain of Lévi-Straussian 'hoaxes' illustrates something regrettable about the work of the master of 'structural anthropology': Lévi-Strauss has developed an excellent method of analysis; but he does not know how (or does not *wish*) to apply it. An experienced practitioner as long as he is endeavouring to isolate 'elements' or to seek out 'correspondences' at different levels of social reality, he goes off course as soon as he tries to proceed to *synthesis*. Indeed, at this stage, his (conscious or unconscious) ideological presuppositions nearly always compel him to fit everything into a Procrustean bed which represents his dogmatically preconceived elementary structure.

In a dossier dedicated to him last year, the editors of the *Magazine littéraire* (November 1971) stated that 'there are two possible readings of Lévi-Strauss, according to which he pursues either a definite scientific investigation or a philosophical anthropology.' But in the same dossier, Mrs. Catherine Backès-Clément writes: Lévi-Strauss' work 'is doubtlessly a scientific work first of all [...]. To attempt an approach of a literary and philosophical type would be to go against the explicit intentions of the author.' This contradiction should not surprise. What is irritating about Lévi-Strauss' works is precisely the 'explicit intentions of the author,' who wishes to be a man of science, opposing himself to the supremely ambiguous character of his discourse, in which science and ideology intermingle inextricably. Einstein derived a conviction from his discoveries in the existence of *his own* god, and did not tire of telling us so. But his ideological conclusions remained clearly beyond the bounds of his scientific work; no confusion was possible. With Lévi-Strauss, on the contrary, this confusion is *de rigueur*. To the extent that we might ask ourselves if the author of *Mythologies* does not aim as much — even above all — to pass off an ideological merchandise under the guise of a scientific proposal.

In fact, the *ideological objective* that Lévi-Strauss proposes to his contemporaries is the *exit from history*. 'History may lead to anything,' he has asserted, 'provided you get out of it.'[9] This proposal, it is true, was only formulated with respect to History as a science. But in reality,

---

9 *The Savage Mind*, tr. (University of Chicago Press, 1966), p. 262. — Tr.

it constitutes a *Leitmotiv* that governs the entire *oeuvre*, and aims, beyond historical science, to 'become historic' itself.

Exiting History

Lévi-Strauss also has a habit of playing with the ambiguities of language and style. When asked to 'explain himself,' as in the case of his controversy with Mr. Jean-Paul Sartre, he defends himself from being a disparager of history. He asserts that historical research remains foreign to his preoccupations, which does not keep him from acknowledging the legitimacy and eventual soundness of a historical science. On occasion, he even indulges in meditations that seem to establish a link between his history and his work. 'Coming to the evening of my career,' he writes, 'the last image that myths leave me and, through them, that supreme myth that recounts the history of humanity...' But make no mistake. Lévi-Strauss is quite convinced of having situated his work beyond History; of having 'exited History.' Moreover, in *The Savage Mind*, he states that 'history is a method with no distinct object corresponding to it.' This leads him to urge us to 'reject the equivalence between the notion of history and the notion of humanity which some have tried to foist on us with the unavowed aim of making historicity the last refuge of a transcendental humanism.'[10]

It is of course unclear how it would be possible to deny a 'human transcendence' always written into the reality of things, to the extent that this 'transcendence' is explicitly linked to the notion of history. Certainly, man is a living being; and life amounts, in the last analysis, to the physicochemical. But just as life *transcends* the physicochemical (whose laws it *suspends*), so man 'transcends' life, being confronted with a 'tragic destiny' in the Nietzschean sense of the term (if only because he has 'no instincts,' as Lévi-Strauss himself has recognised). We may admit nonetheless (and we do indeed believe) that it is possible for man to 'exit history' by giving himself, once and for all, the

---

10   Ibid. — Tr.

'instincts of the species.' Some might even desire this 'evasion.' It does not change the fact that, *actually*, man is *in history*. His eventual decision to 'exit' it can be understood only as a *historic act* (the *last*, to be precise), and therefore *within history*.

In this light, any science of man must be historical. It is no doubt the case, as Lévi-Strauss recalls, that 'historical facts are no more *given* than any others,' and that 'It is the historian, or the agent of history, who constitutes them by abstraction, and as though under the threat of an infinite regress.'[11] But the *historical fact* is peculiar, beside other 'facts,' in that is it constituted by a thought or an action of man taking man himself (or, more precisely, *another* man) for an object. Better still, man does not *constitute himself as man* except in historical fact.

Anthropology will struggle to *radically* distinguish man from primate, his immediate ancestor, if it does not take account, first of all, of the *historicity* of the former: that is, the presence in the first human societies of the created tool, the concrete manifestation of a 'gesture' whose correlate is the 'word.'[12] In this sense, *hominization* may be considered the first 'historic fact,' by means of which *man constituted himself as man*, and plunged into History, taking responsibility for his future. Contrary to what the Bible claims, 'Adam' and 'Eve,' walking in Eden, did not constitute the first human couple. They were still primates. Moreover, they were not 'banished' from Eden: they left deliberately. They abandoned the *absolute state of nature* (the 'state of innocence') in order to become humans. Was it a 'sin'? There is no doubt that Lévi-Strauss, with the Bible, with Marx and Freud, take this first 'historic fact' (and all history that follows it) to be entirely *evil*, like

---

11 Ibid., p. 257. — Tr.

12 The presence of the tool does not alone suffice to determine the 'presence of man.' A tool may have been *given* naturally; its 'fabrication' may have been written *unchangingly* into the instinct of the species. Man is only distinguished by the *created* tool: that is, the tool imagined, *projected* and realized beyond 'natural' givens. Ultimately, an *initial* fabricated tool cannot assure us in this regard. It is necessary to find a *second* tool, transformed by its relation to the first.

an 'error' in need of repair. To their eyes, history takes the appearance of an 'exit from Paradise.' Contrarily to Freud, who cultivated pessimism and a certain snobbery, though entirely in accord with Marx and the Bible, Lévi-Strauss remains optimistic. He asserts that one can exit history and 'return to Paradise' — a rather terrestrial Paradise, in which men will be *happy*, since nothing happens.

A Historical Animal

Lévi-Strauss then offers us the Bororo societies of the Amazon as an example, primitive societies in the process of disappearance (as a result of the civilization of the white man — history's incorrigible troublemaker). To his eyes, these societies have the merit of having tried to 'exit History,' and of having succeeded.

Mr. Edmund Leach has remarked that 'Again and again in Levi-Strauss' writings we keep coming back to this point. ... "In what way is the Culture of Homo sapiens inseparable from the Nature of humanity?"'[13] In fact, Lévi-Strauss' reasoning is absurd. The existence of European civilization leads him immediately to assert that culture and nature can be dissociated. And the real question that his work attempts to answer is not of a theoretical, but of a rather *practical* order. It is as follows: In what way might culture — that of western man — return to nature?

Let there be no mistake that this distinction between 'culture' and 'nature' is at the origin of everything that is or might be *ambiguous* in Lévi-Strauss. *For there is no possible distinction between the Culture and the Nature of man.* Consequently, his having postulated such a separation (and of postulating it *in practice*) reveals itself to be a strategic fiction: in this way, Lévi-Strauss codifies his discourse and finds it possible to present ideological value-judgements as scientific results.

It is difficult to believe in Lévi-Strauss' 'naïveté.' His 'strategic fiction' has every appearance of a calculated ruse. This is at least the

---

13   Op. cit., p. 131. — Tr.

impression one might get from reading the passages in which Lévi-Strauss, perhaps giving into scientific vanity, implies that he knows very well where the truth lies. So it is that he insists on the fact that 'man has no instincts,' such that, according to him, 'social conventions much take the place that instincts hold among the animals.' But let us not play with words. To say that 'man has no instincts' amounts to saying that man has no nature. 'Having instincts' means dealing *automatically*, thus with full confidence, with oneself and with the environment (the *Umwelt*) of the species with which this 'self' is faced. The animal knows: he understands perfectly the right answers to the questions posed by his *existence*. He knows, as Lévi-Strauss emphasises, what food suits him and where to go to find it. Man, once weaned, does not know. He understands, in himself, neither questions nor answers. He must learn them. He is thus untethered from the constraints of the species only *negatively*, in the form of a *limit*; and it is in this regard that he has no nature.

This perspective also has its reverse. While having no *actual* nature, man has access to a practically unlimited number of *potential* natures. He is 'all the animals,' but only in potency. This stems from his extraordinary plasticity; from his capacity for adaptation, in terms of which his intelligence is properly defined; and this is the reason that we can see in him a 'sick animal.' Being contradictory, these instincts mutually paralyse one another. Where an animal hears only *one* question, requiring *one* programmed response (written into the 'programme' of the species), man hears an infinity of questions, requiring an infinity of possible responses, which mutually exclude (paralyse) one another precisely. In order to *exist*, man is therefore required to *choose* one question, one answer, one nature, one instinct from among (and in opposition to) all *possible* others. The *nature* that he has chosen, and that he realised by 'selecting' one instinct and 'repressing' the others, is culture. In other words, culture is the nature man gives himself by a decision he makes. *It is human nature constituted as such, and thus realized.* And this decision is the *first 'historic fact.'* Primate becomes man by entering into History.

In light of these considerations, the 'fundamental question' posed by Lévi-Strauss can easily be deciphered. When Lévi-Strauss asks how 'the culture of Western man, dissociated from nature, might reintegrate itself into it,' he really asks: How might Western culture be *led* to follow the example of Bororo societies, folding in on itself and 'exiting History'?

Creation and Repetition

There is nothing arbitrary about our interpretation. It suffices, in order to prove it, to turn to another distinction, also fundamental, that Lévi-Strauss makes between 'hot societies' and 'cold societies.' The latter, he writes, are those that 'react to the *historical condition*' by trying to '*ignore*' it, and by 'trying, with an adroitness that we underestimate, to render as permanent as possible those states that they consider *first* in their development.' As for 'hot societies,' of which the western world is the most typical representative, these are those that 'accept' the historical condition 'willingly or unwillingly, and, with the consciousness they attain, augment its consequences, for themselves and for other societies, to enormous proportions.'

Lévi-Strauss then presents cold societies, which he more generally calls primitive, as shining, even heartwarming examples of fidelity to tradition, to permanence, and to 'Being.' Borrowing the description given by T. G. H. Strehlow of the everyday customs of the northern Aranda, he adopts this conclusion: 'The native follows tradition blindly: he clings to the primitive weapons used by his forefathers, and no thought of improving them ever enters his mind.'[14] But this seductive homily plays with appearances. It implies a quite fallacious definition of tradition. With a certain dexterity, Lévi-Strauss here

---

14   *The Savage Mind*, op. cit., p. 235. — Tr.

confuses letter and spirit, *acte* and *fait*,[15] the gesture and its effect. For by continuing to use their 'primitive weapons,' the Aranda do not respect but *betray* their forefathers. Indeed, they *repeat* where their forefathers improvised or invented; they *churn the mud* where their ancestors advanced; they *seek refuge* in a certain world where their forefathers, defying the unknown, opened the doors of a new world. 'Faithful to tradition,' these Aranda are merely *residual fossils* of the history of their forefathers.

It goes without saying that, from Lévi-Strauss' ideological perspective, man has no reason to desire to go *beyond this decision*, by which he has found a Nature in Culture, to the extent that his *existence* is now assured. A perfectly legitimate assessment, of course, if it remains a value-judgement (to which others, no less 'legitimate,' are opposed). An erroneous judgement, on the other hand, if it is presented as a logical consequence of the genuine 'meaning' of the decision by which culture is founded. Indeed, we might say, to return to what has already been indicated with regard to tradition, that culture is (and remains) culture only on condition that it reproduce not the *created fact* but the *creative act* by which it is established. Culture is constituted by a decision which is also a renunciation; by the exaltation of one instinct which is also the repression of other instincts. In man's case, the 'negativity of nature' remains nonetheless real, since the *first decision* implies in itself the necessity of unceasingly *further decisions* between contradictory options. So it is because he has 'entered into history' that man's 'freedom' is always preserved. Relative freedom with respect to its *object*: man can only decide between options determined by his past. But freedom with respect to its *subject*: man can also decide, in an *ultimate decision*, to renounce this freedom which is his own (and which is always on the table) by 'exiting' history in order to 're-enter' the species.

---

15 Cf. the distinction in French law between (willed) '*actes juridiques*' and (un-willed) '*faits juridiques*.' — Tr.

Project, Myth, Decision

The act by which a culture is founded always represents a *project*, an idea which expresses and poses a principle, a *myth*, which historical development is called to realise. No doubt from the 'conscious' perspective of that which poses the *principle*, this latter might appear to be accomplished in itself as a goal pursued and already attained. But once posed, the principle then manifests its character as a *project* aiming at a goal no longer attained, and which must be pursued.

Moreover, once the goal attained is recognised as *ultimate*, it loses its objective signification; and the necessity arises of a *new constitutive choice*. This eventuality is permanent: at any moment the goal attained may be felt and considered to be *sufficient* by an individual or collective human consciousness. In this case society turns upon the last moment of History that it has seen, and does nothing but *reproduce* it. Thus condemning itself eternally to 'repeat' its past, it *exits the present* by 'exiting history.' It becomes what Lévi-Strauss calls a 'cold society.'[16]

'Cold societies' ought really to be called *cultural broken branches*. They are *arrested* societies which, like some species or other, do not evolve except by chance exterior "events" under the pressure of 'events' external to themselves. They are therefore at the mercy of every change in environment not foreseen by their 'programme.' In short, they can only subsist on condition that they not run into the very history from which they exited. It is for this reason that contact with Western societies proves fatal for 'cold' (primitive) societies. For the white man, even today, still represents history. *He is history.* And it is for this reason that the 'exit from history' can be called into question: individuals and groups of individuals can be recovered for history by more historically advanced cultures. We live today in a world in which 'tepid societies' wash *back from their past towards the present of Western societies*, to

---

16   This is not to say, of course, that one ought to advocate for any old 'cult of progress,' an ideological rite that, by a subtle twist of Hegelian reason assimilated by Marx, disguises the same old aspiration to an *ultimate goal*: opening the doors to the court in which the Last Judgement of History is held.

which the majority of their denizens, without even realizing it, attempt to resemble and identify themselves.

In *The Savage Mind*, Lévi-Strauss writes:

> [T]he first difference between magic and science is therefore that magic postulates a complete and all-embracing determinism. Science, on the other hand, is based on a distinction between levels: only some of these admit forms of determinism; on others the same forms of determinism are held not to apply. One can go further and think of the rigorous precision of magical thought and ritual practices as an expression of the unconscious apprehension of the truth of determinism, the mode in which scientific phenomena exist. In this view, the operations of determinism are *divined* and *made use of* in an all-embracing fashion before being *known* and *properly applied*, and magical rites and beliefs appear as so many expressions of an act of faith in a science yet to be born.[17]

In this passage, in which he seeks to rehabilitate 'magical thought,' Lévi-Strauss seems to recognise, implicitly, at least, that this mode of thought is situated at an inferior *level of consciousness*: it is 'an act of faith in a science yet to be born'; a thought not yet conscious of its 'determinism.' Now in this territory one may go further still. Since the savage mind is *logical*, why not admit that non-degenerate 'magic' is an genuine 'science' and, by the same token, a practical wisdom ('knowhow')[18] aiming to produce certain *effects* by mobilising adequate *causes*? For magic is not a *game*. No more is it an 'act of faith' in a coming science (unless one consider Newtonian theory to be an 'act of faith' in a coming Einsteinian science). In reality magic only takes on the aspect of a game once it has *degenerated*, which befalls it precisely in those 'cold societies' so dear to Lévi-Strauss. And its degeneration consists in its forgetting its true *object* and attempting to apply it where its method is unsuited.

---

17 Ibid., p. 11. — Tr.

18 English in the original. — Tr.

'Authentic' Magic

Let us explain. To define magic, Lévi-Strauss cites Evans-Pritchard:

> If a buffalo gores a man, or the supports of a granary are undermined by termites so that it falls on his head, or he is infected with cerebro-spinal meningitis, Azande say that the buffalo, the granary and the disease are causes which combine with witchcraft to kill a man. witchcraft does not create the buffalo and the granary and the disease for these exist in their own right, but it is responsible for the particular situation in which they are brought into lethal relations with a particular man. ... Of these causes the only one which permits intervention is witchcraft, for witchcraft emanates from a person.[19]

These few lines evince perfectly what 'degenerate' magic is, but also what *authentic* magic must originally be. The degenerate magic of the Azande invents an erroneous cause (witchcraft) which, as such, is susceptible to corrective intervention (counter-witchcraft). It applies itself, therefore, to a non-existent object. Contrarily, 'authentic' magic ('scientific,' if you like) would be that which applies itself to a real, clearly perceived object. This would not be the environment, but rather the human *psyche*. Magic would then aim to refine a *psycho-technology* which would not pretend to correct events but quite simply to put man in a condition, either to withstand without excessive pain the hostile pressures of a universe that he does not govern, or to unleash certain of his instincts, while repressing others, in order to make him fit (or fitter) for some enterprise or other. With this type of magic man manipulates himself. He gives himself a 'chosen nature' and completes his hominization.

'Lacking instincts' and deprived of an 'actual nature,' but making use of 'potential natures,' man is no longer confronted by a *species-environment* but with a genuine universe, which is the sum of all possible species-environments. To all the questions, to all the problems that this ever-changing world throws at him, man must give a response.

---

19   Ibid. — Tr.

That is to say that he must, according to circumstances, *recover the 'species-nature'* that has the adequate response. He must, in short, know with which animal to identify. For, in a way, animals reveal to him their secrets and their *art*. As their instincts are immutable, they represent to his eyes an infinity of *living responses*. Man is their pupil. His *instinctual plasticity*, his ability to extend his body and to correct its 'deficiencies' by means of fabricated tools, permit him to become 'the animal he wishes to be.' A ritualized process of exaltation or repression of urges (self-suggestion, above all, due to the ritual use of drugs, to rhythmic dance, to 'repetition') provides the *information* (inspired by the imitation of a certain number of observed models) thanks to which he breaches the dyke separating his *'natural' nothingness* from his *'cultural' existence*. Thus, 'authentic' magic is nothing other than the knowhow[20] of *human self-domestication*, which is organized by a science stemming from a reflection upon the *'savoir-faire'* of animal nature.

Magic degenerates, as we have said, once it claims to pertain to relations other than those between consciousness and *psyche*. This degeneration can take place in two ways. In the case of the Azande cited by Lévi-Strauss, magical practice is applied to a relation between man (as living being) and the world (as event) under the purely imaginary pretext of the human *psyche*'s participation in the causes of the event (witchcraft). In other cases, a *psyche* of a human type is attributed to the world itself (taken as a thing) and to observed *agents* in the world, which one seeks vainly to influence, etc.... But let us not pretend than man originally used magical practice only in circumstances when it 'suited' him to use it. The simple matter of attributing a *psyche* to the world and to exterior agents certainly constituted, at the very beginning of the human adventure, an excellent means by which indirectly to shore up man's self-assurance, to render him more confident in his power with respect to his environment. In order to find the strength to *exist*, man must make use of every means at his disposal. In fact,

---

20 English in the original. — Tr.

degeneration begins, from a historical perspective, when *reflection* upon magic gives rise to unwarranted conclusions and leads to an entirely *erroneous* 'cosmological' *theory*. Contrarily, where such a *reflection* permits him to isolate the true terms of the 'magical relation,' man acquires a precise awareness of himself and of the position he occupies in the living world. He becomes, from then on, the *domesticator of the living world*.

The Neolithic Revolution

Having learnt what moves himself, man then tried to 'make' animals move according to his desires and his needs. As concerned the 'social animals,' he offered himself to assume a leading role in this regard, and so to take the place of the chief of the troupe. In the same way, those who attained a superior *level of consciousness*, thanks to a correct reflection on the 'magical relation,' offered themselves as an *élite* with respect to society and asserted their own *sovereignty*. Religion then constituted the ideological system which would allow society to be 'bound' and the mass to be submitted to a given influence. And this is the *Neolithic Revolution*.

The contrast, at this moment, became brutal. Magic represented the 'science' and the technical *'savoir-faire'* of the societies of the predators of nature. Thanks to magic, man perfected his auto-domestication and progressively assured his primacy in the Animal Kingdom. Beginning in the Neolithic, society acquired a new dimension, which translated into a psycho-social cleavage. The old dimension—that is, the old mentality—subsisted at the level of the *mass*; while the new was the province of the *élite*. Two types of men now found themselves thrown together, no longer only from the point of view of individual psychology but rather from the *social* perspective. In parallel to the domestication of the living world (taken as a whole) by man, the 'domestication' of the mass was effected by the *élite*; of *magical* man by *religious* man.

This 'transition' that the Neolithic Revolution constituted, and which the historical period currently in the process of completion (with the 'transition' to the domestication of the material) represents, assumes a fundamental importance. It is not difficult to discern here, in a more realist form, what the Bible calls 'the expulsion from earthly Paradise'; Karl Marx, the end of 'primitive communist society'; Sigmund Freud, 'the death of the father'; Lévi-Strauss, 'the separation of nature and culture.'

This period is all the more interesting now that we possess an authentic and significant testimony on this subject, which Mr. Georges Dumézil has the immense merit of having 'recovered,' clarified and astutely interpreted. This is the original Indo-European myth of the 'society of the gods,' a myth also 'inherited' by the Romans, the Aryans, the Celts, the Greeks to a lesser extent, but preserved among the Germans in the form of the tale of the 'war between the Aesir and the Vanir.'

War of the Gods

In Germanic mythology, it is from the conflict between the Aesir and the Vanir that the harmonious society of the gods is born, organised according to the trifunctional principle, which clearly reflects, in an idealised form, original Indo-European society (or more exactly the *project* that their inheritors strove to realise). Much speculation of a 'historicist' type has tried to see in the Aesir and Vanir 'deified' representations of two *different peoples*, one living by hunting and gathering, the other by agriculture, which first fought then superimposed one another. Such is not my view, for reasons too long to give here. Besides, the question is not especially important to our present discussion. What is essential is that the Aesir and Vanir represent two *different ways of life*: on the one hand, an ancient tradition, that of the *big-game hunters*; on the other, a new, that of the *producers*, who may have infiltrated Indo-European societies by acculturation.

According to the 'legend,' it is Gullveig ('gold-drunkenness'), a goddess of the Vanir, who is the cause of the war. Sent into the land of the Aesir, there she introduces, in effect, the 'power of gold' and, by the same token, discord. In the conflict that follows, the Aesir are beaten precisely on account of their divisions; and the Vanir invade their territory (Asgard, the 'fortress of the Aesir'). However, at the end of the day it is the Aesir who prevail. Their chief, Odin–Wotan, imposes peace. This result may surprise and appear to contradict the tale. Now, the reason for Wotan's 'victory' is very simple. Odin–Wotan, who is the 'master of the runes,' is the *magician-god* par excellence. He '*domesticates*' the Aesir by means of magic.

In the unified society formed by the Aesir and Vanir once the war is over, the first assume the noble function: the *sovereign* function (Wotan) and the *warrior* function (Thor). The Vanir, for their part, assume the economic function (Njörðr, Freyr and Freyja): they are charged to produce society's riches. We are therefore faced with a genuine social contract, marvellously illustrating the *nature* of the Neolithic Revolution. For the sovereign function has two aspects: a magical and *constrictive* aspect, which we might call *political*, since it serves a repressive purpose; and an also magical but *benevolent* aspect, which manifests itself through protection, and which we might call *religious*. Here it is rather a matter of the double aspect of one and the same function, of one and the same reality. Indeed, we are convinced, contrary to Mr. Dumézil, that the Sovereign God was originally but one *Dyeus Pater*, who was only 'redoubled' (mainly among the Indo-Aryans, and partially among the Germans) at a later date, when, in the *society of men*, the two functions were separated, distinguishing two 'castes.' The Aesir then claimed for themselves the role of 'domesticators of the mass' (sovereign function, warrior function), a role implying and requiring *protection*; while the Vanir found themselves entrusted with the 'domestication of nature,' the production of goods.

Higher Consciousness

What is striking about the 'arrangements' imposed by Wotan is the fact that sovereignty is not attributed to *technicians*, to the 'domesticators of life,' but rather to those to use a 'higher magic': that is, a magic pertaining *as much* to the 'domesticators of life' as to representatives of the mass man, to the 'other gods.' We now see that the myth contains an *implicit teaching* based upon a specifically Indo-European value-judgement which wills that man's *authenticity* reside in his capacity to 'take himself in hand,' to 'speak' and to 'act,' rather than to 'be spoken' and to 'be acted.' From the moment that man becomes conscious of this aptitude — that is, from the moment he reflects upon his powers of self-domestication — a *higher consciousness* arises, which strives immediately to realise itself as such in social fact. To the generic (and spontaneous) subject-man of magical action exercised upon himself is now added the specific (and conscious) subject-man of magical action exercised upon *another man.* the distinction between the mass and the *élite* arises at the same instant. It is this that Lévi-Strauss intends, by arguing for a pretended 'separation between culture and nature,' to condemn.

This introductory text, a guide to the Wagnerian *Tetralogy* and its author, is the ideal complement to *Wagner, Nietzsche and the Superhumanist Myth*, which assumes a certain awareness with the composers works and themes. This analysis appeared in a special monographic double edition of *Nouvelle École* — no. 30 (autumn 1978) and no. 31–2 (spring 1979) — in no. 30, to be precise, which also collected a number of essays later developed and filled out into the abovementioned essay. It is at home at the end of this second part, 'Roots,' since *The Ring of the Nibelung* marks the arrival of the superhumanist myth. Indeed, Richard Wagner's work revives and transfigures Europeans' earliest memories, and aims, in Heideggerian terms, at a 'more originary origin' for European civilization faced with the challenge of the 'third man.'

4

Introduction to
The Ring of the Nibelung

ONE CAN HARDLY 'retell' the *Ring*—still less can retelling it give even the most fleeting sense of its exalting beauty, of the enchanting touch of its breath, of the hight of its world-vision. This observation, which goes for any literary masterpiece, is especially true in the case of *The Ring of the Nibelung*, a *total* artwork which cannot be grasped simply by reading the poem or libretto, but which *must be seen to be understood*, and only in the right place, which is Bayreuth. The 'summary' you are about to read therefore aims only to offer the French 'spectator' a sort of *programme*, which will be especially useful if he has no German,[1] as well as a quick, brief *guide* to aid comprehension of the mythic symbols and allegories through which tragedy *represents* on the stage the Eternal Becoming and Eternal Return which are the history of the gods and of man. At a time when more effort than ever is being spent to falsify and to 'recover' Richard Wagner's work, to the extent of setting up a 'new Bayreuth' against the Bayreuth of tradition established by his wife Cosima, this 'programme-guide' might even be considered necessary by those who refuse to bend to the mendacious *fashion* of a civilization going to the dogs.

---

[1] Wagner's music-dramas are always sung in German.

Prelude to *The Rhine-Gold*

How to *speak* of the birth of the world of gods and heroes? Only music can express the unsayable, speak of the inconceivable. Even before the curtain lifts on the *Ring's* first scene, there is already a sound, mysterious and faceless, unique and fundamental: kept to the contrabasses, who hold it in pedal-point for thirty-six bars, it represents the voice of the Elemental, of the universe itself, which no reason can encompass. It is the voice of the cold, still waters where the *Eddas* find the giant Ymir lying as if in the maternal fluids, whose body will one day be dismembered by the gods to make a *world* for all living things. It is the voice of the very waters that the birth-philosophy of the Greeks made the 'principle' of all things. First, this sound is absolutely alone for four bars. Perhaps it is there for all eternity, for the immeasurable duration of an utterly empty moment. Then another sound joins it: over E-flat stands the fifth; then, a while later, the octave; and then, with an ever more sustained rhythm, all the other natural harmonics in the order established by nature...

This perfect accord designates the 'present': the *first present*. We embark upon Eternal Becoming, on *history*. Rhythm, harmony, melody take shape. The undulating melody amplifies; its palpitations are those of life itself; it enters everything with a slow, impetuous *crescendo*. At last, it breaks: we are in the shining depths of the Rhine and three water-nymphs, daughters of the river-father, play carelessly round the rock where rests the gold they guard. *Incipit tradoedia*.

The Rhine-Gold

Thanks to music, we can *live through* the birth of the world; but we can also take a fantastical shortcut through a whole epoch of indeterminable duration. If we imagine the events as a 'series' forming a parabola, when the curtain rises on *The Rhine-Gold's* first scene, unveiling the depths of the great river, the adventure of gods and men has already reached its climax: the moment we are ready to come to life is the moment the fall begins, takes shape, when the 'tragedy' is staged. Indeed, we have leapt over the birth of the giants and the birth of the gods; we have left the dismemberment of Ymir behind us, along with the long struggle of Wotan and the Æsir to impose order on things, and the war against the Vanir and the subsequent peace, and the birth of man and the organization of his society by Heimdall, the 'first' of the Æsir. All that happened in time immemorial. Now, out of the naïve and joyous singing of the three Rhine-Maidens, irrupts the abortively gracious but inevitably grating cry of dwarf Alberich, the hideous Nibelung. Alberich wants to seduce one of the water-nymphs — it does not matter which — to satisfy his thirst for pleasure; but one after the other, the Maidens undress and mock him with the innocent cruelty of beauty and youth. Naïve, they muddle sexual appetite with love — and when the 'kiss of the sun' pierces the waves to awaken the 'eye of the gold,' they do not fear to reveal their secret: for only he who renounces love can steal the gold and, with this gold which is *power*, achieve world-domination![2]

Alberich, enraged by the Maidens' refusal to bend to his desire, does not hesitate: if love is denied him, he will have the power of the gold and the luxuries it procures. And the dwarf snatches the precious metal from the rock. Immediately, the Maidens's desperate flight announces a universal misfortune: the gold, that sacred treasure under the Rhine which was the guarantee of a *just distribution* of the earth's riches according to the *value* of every living thing, has fallen into unworthy, egotistical hands. Universal *harmony*, which love alone had guaranteed and preserved, has been broken.

Alberich's dream of power and domination is echoed — from the mountain heights where Valhalla, fortress of the Æsir, stands newly built — by Wotan's dream: the dream of the Black Elf by the dream of the Elf of Light. For Wotan also aspires to absolute power, which for him would be the 'manhood's honour' and guarantee of 'endless

---

2   *Wagner's Ring of the Nibelung*, tr. And ed. Stewart Spencer and Barry Millington (London: Thames and Hudson, 2013), p. 65, ff. — Tr.

renown.'³ According to his plan, Valhalla is the means of this power. To build it, Wotan employed the giants Fafner and Fasolt, brute natural forces which even his mind requires to force matter into new forms. Now Valhalla has been built; and at its foot, Wotan readies himself to take possession of it. But he has forgotten (or pretends to have forgotten) that with every right comes a corresponding duty — and that he had promised the giants a reward in return for their labour: Freya, goddess of Love and Eternal Youth. His wife, Fricka, fearing for her sister Freya, reminds him of his promise and scolds him for the lightness of his 'contract' and his inconsideration for woman and love. But Wotan does not listen to Fricka. He had only made his 'contract' in play: Fafner and Fasolt, he thinks, would not know what to do with the gentle Freya; they would be happy with a different reward, which he engages Loge, the wise counsellor, to find.

Wotan is mistaken. The giants, crossing paths with Freya, terrified and overwhelmed, insist upon the price fixed for their work and will not agree to change it. They also dream of subverting world-order by taking from the Æsir the means of their eternal youth, along with Freya and her golden apples.

Meanwhile, Loge arrives. Wotan counts on him to make the giants 'see sense.' But Loge resists the insistences of the Elf of Light. He has promised nothing; guaranteed nothing; his job is simply to consider means to 'solve' the problem arising from the 'contract.' Now, this turns out to be impossible: for nothing in the world is worth as much for man as 'woman's delights and worth.'⁴ Only the Nibelung Alberich — and only he! — believes the gold is worth more than 'woman's favours';⁵ and he has stolen the gold from the Rhine Maidens, who plead for Wotan's aid. Loge himself has only come to inform the god of their plea. In fact, the Machiavellian Loge, with his apparent disinterest

---

3   Ibid., p. 70. — Tr.

4   Ibid., p. 79. — Tr.

5   Ibid., p. 80. — Tr.

in Wotan's situation, has achieved the outcome he had hoped for: hearing him speak, the giants pricked up their ears and, concerned by Alberich's new power, decide to give up Freya in exchange for the Nibelung's treasure. And they carry the goddess with them, arranging to meet with Wotan on the morrow. As the giants leave, the gods sense suddenly, and with dread, that they have begun to age. Indeed, that day they had not eaten Freya's apples of eternal youth. This spurs Wotan to accept Fafner and Fasolt's proposition.

Wotan and Loge then descend into the subterranean abysses of Nibelheim, the den of the dwarves. By one of Loge's ruses, they take Alberich prisoner and bring him (and the gold) back to the foot of Valhalla. Meanwhile, Alberich had made the Rhine-Gold into a magical ring, while his brother Mime had made, according to his instructions, a helmet giving the power to shift into any shape, even to turn invisible. Once Wotan has forced the ring from him — whose power Wotan knows — Alberich, as he leaves, in impotent rage, casts a dreadful curse: the ring will be fatal to whomever possesses it.

The giants arrive at the meeting-point with Freya. Fasolt, who is giving up the goddess reluctantly, asks that enough gold be piled up to hide Freya entirely. But there is not enough gold and Fasolt can see Freya's eye through a remaining chink. He then claims the ring, which is on Wotan's finger. The latter refuses; though, not having eaten the apples of immortality, he feels youth abandoning him. But suddenly the ground opens and Erda, the *Urmutter*, the Mother of All Things, appears — she who knows 'how all things were [...] how all things are, how all things will be.' She warns him: 'Hearken! Hearken! All things that are — end. A day of darkness dawns for the gods: I counsel you: shun the ring!'[6] Wotan wants to know more but Erda has already vanished. However, Wotan still hesitates. Fricka and the other gods, Donner, Froh, Freya, urge him to give in. then he shakes his spear, as if signifying his decision, plucks the ring from his finger and throws it

---

6   Ibid., p. 112. — Tr.

at Fasolt. Freya is freed. Fafner and Fasolt immediately begin to share out the gold and waste no time in fighting brutally for possession of the ring. At last, Fafner beats Fasolt. A solemn silence falls on the witnesses at this first manifestation of Alberich's curse. Fear and anguish seize Wotan's mind, who has already made a resolution to descend to the subterranean depths to seek Erda's counsel. Dark and threatening clouds gather round the peaks. Donner, god of thunder, makes a magical invocation of the thunder, which answers his hammer's call: the storm frees the sky. Froh raises a rainbow that leads to Valhalla. Then a new thought comes Wotan's mind, at once of hope and certainty. For the first time, he sketches in himself a 'grand plan' which he alone understands as yet, but which rings out — as a premonition of the future — in the *Leitmotif*, which is as yet without an 'actual object,' but which we will later identify as that of the sword of the redemptive heroes Siegmund and Siegfried. Happy and newly sure of themselves, the gods head for Valhalla pass the rainbow far above the Rhine, disdaining the distant plea of the water-nymphs, while Loge feels in his heart a desire to leave these divine Æsir who head unwittingly for their destruction, and to turn into a devouring flame that he might destroy those who once tamed and enslaved him.

Let us now examine the meaning of this *re-presentation*. The Æsir, giants and Nibelungen that *The Rhine-Gold* shows us represent the three categories in which Germanic myth, as Robert Saitschick (*Götter und Menschen in Richard Wagners 'Ring des Nibelungen,'* Katzmann, Tübingen, 1957) writes, personifies the three '*levels* of human reality': the sovereign force of a mind that is its own master and that overcomes itself in light of a higher purpose; exuberant physical force created to work but blind incapable of creation; finally, the dark force of an egotistical cleverness that makes a destructive weapon out of everything.

The giants, *urgeschaffen*, created before all other creatures, symbolize 'first mankind' — an as yet 'animal' mankind whose conscient life obeys only the law of the *species*, by which it is limited. In Ymir, from whom they directly descend, the giants represent a continuation of the history of an 'initial' world, long since submerged: the world of a *One* out of whom come the *Two*, from which spring a 'second mankind' for a new history, released from the strictures of the species, endowed with a higher consciousness, but also, by the same token, with a 'consciousness of opposites' shared between the Elves of Light and the Black Elves.

Regarding the Æsir and the Nibelungen, Wagner makes the following judgement: 'all things go their different ways; you can alter nothing' (*'Alles ist nach seiner Art; an ihr wirst du nichts ändern'*), as Wotan says to Alberich (*Siegfried*, II, 1).[7] In which case a morality of 'good' and 'evil' makes no sense. Shaw wanted to see Alberich as the personification of the 'plutocrat,' of the wicked capitalist, and the other Black Elves and the giants as the 'exploited,' the 'wretched of the earth.'[8] More recently, directors influenced by Brecht have decked Wotan and the other Æsir out in a top hat and cigar and transformed Valhalla into a huge factory. This interpretation is not only simplistic: it is also stupid; it leaves gaping 'voids' in a construction whose multiple social categories, 'human' and 'divine,' resist reduction to a Manichaean opposition between 'exploiters' and 'exploited.' Whether we are dealing with gods, giants or dwarves, all, without exception, wish to possess the gold and wish for limitless power. Mime, the 'exploited' *par excellence*, dreams only of seizing Alberich's property. The giants initially wanted Freya as the wages of their labour. They subsequently desired the gold because they desired to dispossess the gods of their ancient power. Alberich renounced love to gain the Rhine-Gold; but, disfavoured by nature, he had no other option. And he could blame Wotan, who 'stole' it: 'If I ever sinned, I sinned freely against myself: but you, you immortal, will sin against all that was, is and shall be.'[9] From his point of view (though he never imagines that by 'cursing love' he taints the one principle able

---

7   Ibid., p. 233. — Tr.
8   Cf. George Bernard Shaw, *The Perfect Wagnerite: A Commentary on the Niblung's Ring* (London: Grant Richards, 1898), pp. 9–10. — Tr.
9   *Wagner's Ring*, op. cit., p. 104. — Tr.

to return a world of opposites to unity) Alberich is quite right. Had not Wotan, the *guarantor of cosmic order*, used trickery to deprive the Black Dwarf of his property? Property which, after all, Alberich had 'conquered' according to an ever-ordained *rule of play*. Alberich still does not know that Wotan, even if only in play, but in light and imprudent play, had also renounced Freya, the symbol of *love* and *woman*.

In the 'present' that *The Rhine-Gold* represents, Wotan's attitude and intentions therefore appear ambiguous, wrapped in mystery. If he is the supreme deity, if he already rules the world, why — as Fricka scolds him — does he want to 'enhance' his 'dominion and power'?[10] Also, the very reasons for his power are also ambiguous. When Wotan refuses to respect the deal he has stricken for the construction of Valhalla, Fasolt challenges him: 'beware: keep your faith with contracts! What you are you are through contracts alone: your power, mark me well, is bound by sworn agreements.'[11] But after all the Æsir oppose the surrendering of Freya, the giant cries: 'You who rule through beauty, you augustly glittering race, how foolish to strive after towers of stone, placing woman's delights in pawn for the sake of castle and hall! We blunderheads toil away, sweating with blistered hand, to win a wife [...] and now you say the deal is invalid?'[12] Everyone is *right* and everyone is *wrong*. If fault there be, Wagner seems to tell us, then they have all committed it, beginning with Wotan, the god-guarantor of world-order. *The Rhine-Gold's* 'present' is therefore that of a decadence that, like all decadence, is already announced and established in the obtuse certainty in 'progress' and 'eternity.' Leaving with his treasure, Fafner, transformed into a dragon, guards his gold in a cave in the depths of the woods, certain that none can find it there. Alberich, trusting in the 'magic' of his curse, is also certain that one day 'his' gold will return to him. As for Wotan: despite Erda's warning, he enters triumphally

---

10 Ibid., p. 71. — Tr.

11 Ibid., p. 74, ff. — Tr.

12 Ibid., p. 75. — Tr.

into Valhalla, convinced that his 'grand plan' with guarantee the reign of the gods for all eternity and restore the threatened world-order. Of course, all are deceiving themselves — even Loge, moreover, who maliciously divines the fall of the gods and plans to betray them, but is unable to see that this end will also be his own, and the world's. Finally, the listener, since he lives in *The Rhine-Gold*'s 'present', cannot but be deceived in turn: he considers Wotan's misstep and the curse of the gold to be the causes of the danger that already hangs over the gods and the world — and perhaps he will sense the end obscurely prophesied by Erda. But in fact in a wider and deeper perspective, the cause of this 'end' is something quite different. It is only later, in the 'present' of the twilight of the gods, that this cause will fully appear.

Therefore, Wagner does not 'judge' characters according to the metric of a morality of good and evil. On the contrary: he stands *beyond good and evil* and, passionately, for what is 'beautiful' and 'noble.' In the representation he offers us, the giants are stupidly, bleakly brutal and detestable. The dwarves, Alberich and Mime,[13] are hideous, odious;

---

13 Commentators, including Guttman and Adorno, have almost always seen Alberich and Mime as 'Jewish caricatures.' Wagner, who was indeed an anti-Semite, did indeed give of the 'Jew' of anti-Semitic convention to the personifications of 'images of man' that he specially detested. According to his intentions, Alberich symbolizes the *Börsenjude* ['stock exchange Jew'], Mime incarnates the *Ghetto-Jude* (and Beckmesser, in the *Master-Singers*, the 'Jewish critic'). Wagner, we know, considered the influence of Jewish elements on German society, and the European societies of his day, to be malign, and fought it tirelessly. He made Judaization responsible for the corruption of a Christianity that, in his eyes, was not at all Jewish originally (being none other, in his view, than the 'modern aspect' of Wotanic religion), just as he saw the underhand work of 'Jewish money-power' in the 'democratic and parliamentary corruption' of European states. For Wagner, the Jews remain the main vector of 'biblical' ideology and the 'Judaic principle' in European societies, the author of the *Ring* differing in this respect from Nietzsche, himself a ferocious opponent of 'Judaism,' but according to whom the Jews of his time simply aspire to 'assimilate' fully and thereby to cease to be Jews. Similarly, if Nietzsche, unlike Wagner, condemns Christianity utterly and irrevocably [see *Wagner, Nietzsche and the Superhumanist Myth* — Ed.], it is because he assimilates the principles of Christianity and Judaism entirely (while

their revolt and their hypocritical surrender reveal their 'slave-souls.' The *tragic* destiny, marked by the most elevated humanity, is reserved for Wotan — the heroes and heroines of the lineage of the *father-god* bathe in its bright light.

The Valkyrie

Wotan can do nothing against the danger that now hangs over the world. As a sovereign deity whose power relies precisely upon 'contracts,' he can hardly wrest forcibly from Fafner the treasure he has yielded him in a precisely contractual manner. Wotan is prisoner of his 'juridical acts'; his hands are tied. Only a *hero* acting 'freely' — following only his own instincts — who kills the dragon, steals the gold and the ring and returns them to the Rhine-Maidens, can cut the Gordian knot that fate has tied. Wotan's 'grand plan,' symbolized by the *Leitmotif* of the sword, was conceived with that intention, so that a hero can undertake his redemptive mission. Having taken human form under the name 'Wälse,' Wotan has therefore begotten two twins, the Wälsungen Siegmund and Sieglinde, on a mortal girl.

One day, returning from the hunt with his son, he finds his house burnt by his enemies who have also taken his wife and their daughter. Wälse-Wotan then abandons Siegmund, making him this promise: a time will come, the hour of his 'highest distress' (*in höchster Not*), when Siegmund will find an invincible sword that he, his father, has forged for him.

> Wagner only assimilates 'historical Christianity' to Judaism, which forgets Jesus' 'true' teaching). In fact, in the 'eternal Jew' (and in the actual Jew: a projection Nietzsche considered unwarranted in the social context of his own time) Wagner expresses an 'idea of man' and a historical 'principle' which belong entirely to the Judaic Bible and to Christianity, and which, in his view, represent the absolute (and non-dialectical) antithesis of the *Rein-Menschliches* ['purely human'] and of the 'idea of music.' Therefore, in Wagnerian discourse, the word 'Jew' — like the word 'German' — ends up designating a 'pure *metaphysicum*' whose incarnations are everywhere.

When the curtain rises on *The Valkyrie*, the hour of Siegmund's 'highest distress' is approaching. Hated by all, absolutely alienated from the spirit of his times, the young hero heed only his heart in a world whose laws he does not understand. He dreams of love and peace but spreads hatred and war without meaning it. To rescue a young girl, he kills her brothers. He loses his weapon in combat and must take flight, pursued by his enemies. One night, chased by storms, exhausted, he seeks refuge in a house in the heart of the woods. A woman welcomes him. At the first exchange of glances, one devouring passion seizes their souls! Hunding, the man the woman has married against her wishes, enters. Siegmund recounts his adventures; Hunding at once recognizes him as an enemy of his race. (The melody leads us to understand that Hunding belongs to a human lineage begotten by giants.) Hunding offers him hospitality for the night as custom dictates, but challenges him to single combat on the morrow. Lying alone in the hall, Siegmund calls to his father and invokes his promise. The woman, who is none other than his sister Sieglinde, returns to him, having sent Hunding to sleep with a potion. She reveals to him that, on the day of her unhappy marriage, a majestic old man, his father no doubt, embedded a sword in an ash-tree which, he predicts, only the greatest of heroes will be able to draw out. Carried away by passion, brother and sister recognize one another. Siegmund pulls the sword from the ash and names it *Notung*, the 'sword of distress.' He offers it to Sieglinde as a wedding-gift (*als Brautgabe*). Then, vowing one to the other with a call of the blood which is also a call of love, he hurries into the early spring night: 'Let the blood of the Wälsungs blossom!'[14]

Everything falls into place according to Wotan's plan. Now events can only follow the course traced in advance by the god. Wotan orders his favourite daughter, the Valkyrie Brünnhilde, to make Siegmund victorious in his combat against Hunding. But Fricka intervenes: as guarantor of marriage-bonds, she would have the victory for Hunding

---

14 *Wagner's Ring*, op. cit., p. 139. — Tr.

and death for the incestuous adulterer Siegmund. Wotan refuses and, for lack of an argument, reveals his plan to Fricka—the redemptive mission for which Siegmund is destined. But the goddess, standing firm, scolds Wotan for his wilful blindness. How could the Elf of Light have abandoned himself to such delusion? Siegmund is not the 'free hero' Wotan wishes to see in him. His invincibility comes from a magical sword forged by his father: it is Wotan's spurring that urges Siegmund on in his quest; his 'freedom' is in fact a *necessity* of the god's making. Beaten, Wotan gives in. He orders Brünnhilde to give Siegmund the defeat; but the Valkyrie does not understand. She sees her father's immense distress and his despair. Confiding his torment in her, Wotan reveals to her, as well, what his plan had been and how vain it has turned out: 'That other self for which I yearn, that other self I never see; for the free man has to fashion himself—serfs are all I can shape.'[15] Again the god summons the ever-reluctant Valkyrie to complete her mission. But Brünnhilde, coming to the battlefield, has not the heart to defeat Siegmund. She tries to give him the victory. So Wotan intervenes himself: his spear shatters Siegmund's sword, who is killed by Hunding before Sieglinde's eyes.

The Valkyrie, overcome, flees with Sieglinde on horseback. Furious, her father pursues. Brünnhilde seeks refuge with her sisters and decides to wait for Wotan there to allow Sieglinde to escape his wrath in a nearby forest where no man enters—the very forest where Fafner jealously guards his treasure. But Sieglinde does not wish to flee. She wishes to join Siegmund in death. Then Brünnhilde reveals that she carries within her the 'pledge received from [Siegmund]': 'O woman, live for the sake of love! [...] a Wälsung stirs in your womb!'[16] Turning suddenly radiant, Sieglinde now invokes 'the mightiest shelter' (*mit mächtigstem Schutz*);[17] she flees, carrying with her the frag-

---

15 Ibid., p. 152. — Tr.
16 Ibid., p. 176, f. — Tr.
17 Ibid., p. 177. — Tr.

ments of Siegmund's sword which Brünnhilde had gathered from the battlefield. Observing these movements, Wotan chases the Valkyries, who beg him to pardon their sister and warn Brünnhilde of the pain in store for her: deprived forever of her divinity and plunged into deep sleep, she will be married to the first man who happens upon her and awakens her. The Valkyries try to make their father give in, saying that all she has done is to follow his secret will. at first unyielding, the god is soon more and more moved by the pleas of those daughters he most loves, and still more by his own pride. He gives in to the Valkyries' pleas, partially: the sleeping Brünnhilde will be protected by a wall of flame that only the strongest and bravest hero shall be able to breach to wake her and take her for a wife.

Of the Tetralogy's four days, *The Valkyrie* always seems to be the most popular with what is called the general public. Indeed, it is entirely sublime: the emotion is unbearable. The tragic cast of the hero's destiny stripped fully bare; and we are all the more profoundly moved by the interlacing of his destiny with Wotan's. On first sight, the action unfolds at two levels: the 'human' and the 'divine.' In fact, the first is simply the mirror of the second: Siegmund, who, on the announcement of his own death, refuses to follow the Valkyrie to Valhalla, since Sieglinde could not join him there, is an 'earthly' reflection of the god who, compelled to abandon his ultimate delusion, accepts his own end and thereby becomes that *higher consciousness* that 'cares for regeneration.' The sword broken by the god's spear is a premonition and prefiguration of the divine spear broken by the same sword, which, in Siegfried's hands, becomes the instrument of a fate now *willed* by the god himself. For the tragedy of heroes and men only finds its ultimate reality and truth in Wotan's tragedy: in the *consciousness* that *knows* but that *wills* nevertheless.

Therefore, since all is resumed, all is past in Wotan's consciousness — since all the characters of the *Ring* are simply aspects of the *Rein-Menschliches*, of the 'purely human,' which is Wotan — the *Ring* is also, fundamentally, the *psychodrama par excellence*, a drama in which

Wagner's immense genius, with stupefying intuition, has projected all the 'guiding images' (*Leitbilder*) with which psychoanalysis, some decades later, would try to support its theories. Brünnhilde sent to sleep by Wotan is the 'secret will,' the innermost will of the god, his indomitable instinct for life, love, 'duration' and eternity — the instinct we are now wont to call 'it' ('Id,' '*Es*'), if that designation does not strike us as particularly ill-chosen. Likewise, Fricka is the 'image' of what Wotan wishes to become and of what he is becoming — his restrictive 'superego.' Now we can better understand the symbolism of the fire that encircles the sleeping Brünnhilde: Wotan, the psychoanalyst would say, *represses* the will and instinct, which, he knows, can only deceive him, into the unconscious. The fire that encircles Brünnhilde is none other than Loge, the *intellect* that betrays and, once again subjugated, only takes on the instrumental role of censure and censorship. Finally, the 'psychoanalytic' allegory conceals another: the 'historical.' Wotan, who has sacrificed his *innermost will*, who has *repressed* what he most loves in himself — Wotan, who, becoming a 'traveller,' will run tirelessly over the face of the earth to examine the signs of the times — is the very image of the declining pagan world that accepts the 'Christian' mask as a painful necessity. However, his innermost will is not dead forever. It *sleeps* — and its unconscious presence, calling the one who will come to awaken it, is the *very presence of music* in our civilization. The 'end' for which the god waits, so he can instigate a 'regeneration' — the beginning of a *new history* — shall be the ultimate 'effect' of the awakening of the sleeping Valkyrie.

Siegfried

It has been said that, in the grand symphony of the *Ring*, *Siegfried* acts as a sort of *scherzo* — the radiant sunset that follows a stormy evening. In the character of Siegfried, Wagner combines the traits of the mythical dragon-slaying hero with those of another mythic hero dear to folktale — 'the boy who goes into the world to learn fear' — as well as, perhaps most importantly, the traits (and destiny) the hero of an age that has forgotten its past, who seeks it and who only comes to divine it at the moment of his death. As the 'residue' of a primordial god, a solar *Naturgott*, within a new religion, the Siegfried of Wagner's staging of the Wotanic myth remains a 'primordial' hero who has nothing behind him, who is not conscious of any past (who lives only in the *present* of his instincts and passions) and who, as always, kills the dragon only to be killed himself (see *The Wibelungen*)[18] by the dragon's descendants.

Siegelinde, collected by Mime, Alberich's brother, has died giving birth to Siegfried. The Black Elf raises the young boy as his 'father and mother in one' (*Vater und Mutter zugleich*),[19] thinking that one day he will steal Fafner's 'treasure' for him and win him 'world-domination.' But Siegfried does not like Mime; the sight of the birds and beasts of the wood teaches him that the hideous dwarf cannot possibly be his father or mother — that he cannot have begotten him, since every child resembles his parents ('no fish ever crept from a toad!').[20] So, once grown, he makes the Nibelung reveal the truth. He then learns that his father, whose name Mime does not know, was killed in combat, that his mother died giving him life, and that the remains of a sword kept by the dwarf are those of his father's weapon. Siegfried then asks Mime to forge him a new sword from the remains; but Mime's art proves powerless — and the Traveller, who is none other than Wotan, foresees the Nibelung's impending death at the end of a cruel game of riddles. Siegfried forges his sword by himself, while the dwarf maliciously challenges him to gain knowledge of fear. The young hero, who knows no fear, lets himself be led by Mime towards Fafner's cave in order to 'learn' this mysterious feeling, which fascinates him.

In his cave, Fafner, transformed into a dragon, grows old on his treasure: 'What I lie on I own.'[21] Alberich, skulking round the monster's

---

18 Wagner, *Prose Works*, vol. 7, tr. William Ashton Ellis (London: Kegan Paul, Trench, Trübner, 1898). — Tr.
19 *Wagner's Ring*, op. cit., p. 202. — Tr.
20 Ibid., p. 203. — Tr.
21 Ibid., p. 233. — Tr.

lair, is also growing old, waiting for the chance to recover 'his' property. The Traveller passes, provoking the ire of Alberich, who recognizes him as his enemy. The dwarf accuses the god of coveting the gold, of wanting to fix the victory over the dragon for Siegfried. Wotan reassures him: he is not here to act but to witness. It is Mime, his own brother, whom Alberich ought to fear! With joyful scorn, Wotan calls to Fafner and predicts the coming of a hero who will kill him unless he give up his treasure. But Fafner is deaf to this warning — and to Alberich, who promises him his life in exchange for just the ring. The Traveller leaves. Alberich hides behind a rock. Siegfried arrives with Mime, who points him to the dragon's cave before scuttling off. Siegfried sleeps at the foot of a tree. When he awakes, he is alone — and the forest is murmuring gently. As if in a dream, Siegfried wonders what his mother looked like. Then he is distracted by the singing of a bird, which he tries to imitate, first with a reed, then with a trumpet... But he only succeeds in rousing the dragon, who tries to eat him. Siegfried kills Fafner by plunging his blade into his stomach. Licking the monster's burning blood from his fingers, the young hero suddenly understands the bird's song: it is telling him to head into the cave and to take the treasure. He follows this advice. Mime leaves his bolthole to follow Siegfried; but Alberich bars his way, leading to a ridiculous argument where both the brothers claim the right to keep the gold. After which both dwarves go away, while Siegfried reappears with the ring on his finger and the magic helmet on his belt. This time, the bird warns him of Mime who has come to declare his 'love' of Siegfried and invites him to try a reinvigorating potion he has prepared. But now the hero understands the murderous intention behind his lying words (for the potion is poisoned) and strikes the traitor down. Down the bird flies, telling Siegfried to head for the rock circled in flames, which only he who knows no fear can breach. Siegfried follows him overflowing with joy: 'I'll gladly follow your call.'[22]

---

22 Ibid., p. 243. — Tr.

At the foot of a craggy mountain, one stormy night, the Traveller compels Erda with an invocation to wake from her eternal sleep and appear before him. From she whose 'sleep is dreaming, [whose] dreaming is brooding, [whose] brooding is exercise of knowledge,' and on whom he had once begotten Brünnhilde, Wotan wishes to learn 'how can the god overcome his care' (*wie besiegt die Sorge der Gott*).[23] But Erda does not know the answer. Wotan sees that, from now on, the very wisdom of the Mother of All Things declines, bends before a god's will. He, Wotan, no longer fears the gods' end — and it is freely, joyfully that he carries out the decisions he had made in the most savage pain. He vows his inheritance to the hero who has conquered the treasure of the Nibelung and who will very soon be reunited with Brünnhilde. Whatever happens, 'to one who's eternally young, the god now yields in gladness.'[24]

As soon as Erda has vanished, Siegfried appears. He is alone: the bird who has accompanied him so far has left. So the hero asks the Traveller the way to the flame-encircled rock. He tells him of his adventures; but the old man seems to mock him. Scornful and impetuous, Siegfried orders him to get out of his path; and the Traveller reveals that he once broke the very sword the young man holds. They confront one another. Wotan's spear is shattered. 'Go on your way! I cannot stop you!' (*Zieh hin! Ich kann dich nicht halten!*) says the god, before vanishing.[25]

Having breached the wall of flame, Siegfried finds 'in weapons a man' (*im Waffen ein Mann*) sleeping under a tree whose helmet hides his face.[26] Gingerly, he unties and lifts up the stranger's cuirass — and sees that he is in a woman's presence. Suddenly aflame with love, he believes he now knows fear. He embraces Brünnhilde. The magic of a

---

23 Ibid., pp. 255, 257. — Tr.
24 Ibid., p. 258. — Tr.
25 Ibid., p. 264. — Tr.
26 Ibid., p. 265. — Tr.

sacred moment covers the silent height, while the Valkyrie, awake at last, hails the sun and light of day (*Heil dir, Sonne! Heil dir, Licht!*) and bursts with joy on the sight of one she has waited and loved so long ('You yourself were all I thought of [...] before you were begotten').[27] The memory of her lost divinity troubles Brünnhilde for a brief moment; Siegfried's passion frightens the warrior-maiden; then her own passion bursts savagely. Might it be Siegfried's turn to fear? No: the hero has forgotten that feeling which he had hardly glimpsed. An irresistible energy unites the extraordinary pair in a promise of eternal love.

The Twilight of the Gods

Unlike Siegmund, who knew where he came from, who carried the image of his father with him, within himself, Siegfried has no idea of his origins. He knows only that Mime cannot be his 'father and mother'; and he has killed him. No 'necessity' has been carefully allotted him in advance by a god. He is *entirely free*. And Wotan, who has put him to the test to make sure of it, has seen his magic spear, symbol of his power, smashes to pieces. On the other hand, because he has *no past*, Siegfried has *no future* either. In the 'age of Wotan,' his 'primordial' nature makes him a sort of *nihilist* hero, who does not hesitate to destroy the world whose values he does not recognize, but who has no goal of his own. The 'redemption' that he voluntarily guarantees with his death his bound to a *destruction*. It is the necessary but *not sufficient* condition of the '*regeneration* of the world' that Wotan has planned.

Now everything is clear. Wotan's 'fault' and Alberich's and the giants' blameworthy thirst for domination and unending riches are not the *cause* of *Ragnarök*, the fatal twilight of the gods and the world. At most, they determined the time and the manner. But the end was written into things from the beginning. Now, in the 'present' of the *Götterdämmerung* [Twilight of the Gods], we see the truth. At the

---

27 Ibid., p. 268. — Tr.

foot of Yggdrasil, the world-ash, the three Norns feel a sacred terror rising within them. As they weave the thread of Fate, they meditate upon what once was, what is becoming, and what shall be. And this is what their memories show. Before the reign of the gods had begun, before *history* had begun, Wotan went to the spring that rises at the foot of Yggdrasil. He drank its water, gaining *knowledge*, for which the 'price' was one of his eyes. He broke a branch of the world-ash and fashioned it into his spear into which he carved runes of wisdom; and in his hands the weapon became both the guarantee of *contracts* and the tool of his own power. Now we know, from the beginning, why Wotan was willing to sacrifice his eye: to gain both wisdom and power. When Fricka scolded him for pawning Freya to build Valhalla, the Elf of Light answered: 'In order to win you as wife, my one remaining eye I staked that I might woo you: how foolish you are to blame me now [for "gambl[ing ...] love and womanhood's worth"].'[28] If Wotan coveted wisdom and power, it was for *love*—for love of Fricka. Love, the only way to *Erlösung*, 'redemption,' is also the *principle* which always calls an 'end.' In Wagner's eyes, love and death are indissolubly linked: they are the very law of life. In the Wagnerian conception, love is not *caritas* but *eros, geschlechtliche Liebe*, sexual love: the melding and overcoming of complementary opposites originating from a single matrix—reunion that alone allows human creatures to achieve their particular completeness, their particular perfection. And *life*, of which love is the highest law, is perpetual *change*: 'All that lives dies'—so it is and so it *must be*. To be conscious at every moment, without seeking refuge in oblivion or illusion, but nevertheless accepting and affirming life at every moment, is to attain—beyond life itself—the *tragic* dimension of humanity and history: to achieve genuine *humanity*, the 'divinity,' the consciousness that no animal possesses or can possess.

Such a vision of life frightens the primordial deities who are the extension of the 'first man' in the 'age of Wotan.' Once the thread of

---

28 Ibid., p. 72.—Tr.

destiny snaps, announcing the coming of the end of the world, the Norns flee, terrified, into the belly of the earth, into eternal sleep with their mother Erda. For the moment of the end is at hand.

Siegfried has won the ring. He has given as a token of his love to Brünnhilde who has given him knowledge of the 'sacred runes' (*heiliger Runen*) and exhorted him to new heroic endeavours, to new victories. Siegfried then goes out into the world, carried and guided by his exuberant ardour, pledging eternal fidelity to the Valkyrie. But the sky is already darkening. Hagen, son of Alberich, dreams of losing Siegfried and winning back the ring. He spins his web. His half-brother Gunther, King of the Gibichungen, is without a wife since no woman is worthy of him. Hagen cunningly tells him about Brünnhilde, the most marvellous woman in the world (*das herrlichste der Welt*), a woman protected by an unbreachable fire whom Gunther himself could not conquer. Only Siegfried, continues Hagen, can carry off this deed; and no doubt he would agree to do it for Gunther if he were given for wife the lovely Gutrune, the King's sister, who also languishes unmarried.

At that moment, Siegfried arrives at the court of the Gibichungen. As impetuous and naïve as ever, he demands that Gunther become his ally or fight with him. On Hagen's advice, Gutrune offers the hero a potion of love and oblivion to drink. At once, Siegfried falls in love with her and asks her hand in marriage. This potion, like all 'potions' in Wagnerian drama, is only a symbol. Siegfried, the hero 'without a past,' has no *memory*: he lives only in the 'present' (in the actuality of the lived moment, to put it in nonlinear terms). He is endlessly susceptible to his soul's successive impulses. A 'pact' is quickly sealed: Siegfried, whom the magic helmet will give Gunther's appearance, will overcome Brünnhilde's resistance and giver her to the king, to whom he bonds himself in 'blood-brotherhood' — while Hagen, on the pretext of the 'impurity' of his blood, abstains from taking the pledge.

On the mountain heights, Brünnhilde lives in wait of Siegfried's return. Another Valkyrie, her sister Waltraute, appears before her and begs her to return the ring to the Rhine-Maidens in order to save 'both god and world.'[29] Waltraute describes the limitless pain Wotan has been in since he returned to Valhalla with the shards of his spear. Wotan had ordered the warriors gathered in Valhalla to fell the world-ash to make an immense pyre 'around the sacred enclosure'; then he had gathered the parliament of gods in this enclosure. Since then, he is waiting in silence, no longer touching the apples of youth, while limitless terror overwhelms the gods and heroes. But Brünnhilde does not hear this tale: she will never sacrifice the ring, token of Siegfried's love; she will never be stripped of her love, 'though Valhalla's glittering pomp should moulder into dust' (*stürzt' auch in Trümmern Walhalls strahlende Pracht*).[30]

A storm erupts. The flames that enrobe the peaks climb skyward, more furious than ever. A warrior approaches; he breaches them. It is not Siegfried! Approaching Brünnhilde, he calls her to follow him and become his wife. In vain the Valkyrie tries to refuse him. The man bends her to his will and takes the ring from her — without touching her: for *Notung*, Siegfried's sword, stands between the Valkyrie and the one who, true to his word, destines her for Gunther, whose appearance he has assumed.

Before the palace of the Gibichungen, where he is keeping watch, Hagen sees Alberich appear in a dream. The latter, reminding him of the 'injustice' he has suffered, demands vengeance. He tells Hagen to kill Siegfried and steal the ring. Hagen darkly assures him: he has sworn to steal the fatal ring and to keep it for him. On the return of Siegfried, who tells the delighted Gutrune of Gunther's and Brünnhilde's imminent arrival, Hagen is gripped by savage joy. With his horn, Alberich's son calls Gunther's men who rush him, in arms, believing their master threatened by some enemy. With a wicked pleasure, Hagen leaves them uncertain for a while before inviting them to prepare nuptial sacrifices for Siegfried and Gutrune. Very soon, all are reunited — and then

---

29 Ibid., p. 304. — Tr.
30 Ibid., p. 305. — Tr.

realize Hagen's Machiavellian plan. Brünnhilde, who follows Siegfried, frozen in profoundest humiliation, sees Siegfried at Gutrune's side and — at the same instant — hears the news of their imminent marriage. In a flash, the ring on Siegfried's finger reveals to her the overwhelming truth: it was not Gunther but Siegfried who rescued her! Before all assembled, the Valkyrie cries the truth: she denounces the fraud, the betrayal, and reveals herself to have been Siegfried's wife. But he denies it fiercely. He no longer has any memory of his first meeting with Brünnhilde; and when Hagen invites him to swear an oath over the spear, he does not hesitate a moment. Propelled by savage fury, Brünnhilde also vows that she has spoken truly. Siegfried, uncaring, declares her 'sick' and gleefully invites Gunther to 'heal' her. One day, surely, the woman will be grateful for his having won her for the king! Left alone with Hagen and Brünnhilde, humiliated before his people by Siegfried's revelations which have shown the extent of his deception, Gunther hears his half-brother advise him to cleanse his shame in Siegfried's blood. Brünnhilde herself calls for the hero's death in vengeance. Feeble Gunther still hesitates: Siegfried has become his blood-brother; and he is not certain that he has tricked him. He only allows himself to be convinced once Hagen reveals to him the ring's power to gain Gunther world-domination. When Brünnhilde reveals that Siegfried is invincible, invulnerable, and that he can only be felled treacherously by a blow to the back, he decides that Hagen will take care of matters out on a hunt, so Gutrune can be told that Siegfried was killed by a boar. Vengeance is settled. Gunther, Hagen and Brünnhilde solemnly swear: 'So shall it be! May Siegfried fall' (*So soll es sein! Siegfried falle*).[31]

At the foot of a sudden outcrop where the Rhine crosses a forested valley, the Rhine-Maidens sing nostalgically, at the surface of the river, of their lost purity. Suddenly, Siegfried appears. Out hunting, he has lost his way in pursuit of a bear. A mischievous dialogue follows between

---

31   Ibid., p. 330. — Tr.

the hero and the three nymphs. They want Siegfried to gift them the golden ring, which he has with him; but the hero refuses because of the reproach he would get from Gutrune. The Maidens, mocking him, disappear among the waves. When they reappear, Siegfried, vexed, offers them the ring. But now the Maidens do not want it — at least, not before Siegfried hears directly from them the fate that awaits him: if he refuses to surrender the ring, he will die before end of day. Siegfried need only refuse once more to surrender the ring, which he may be able to do out of love, but which he can never do under threat: he has never known fear; he casts off 'life and limb' (*Leben und Leib*) like a clod of earth.[32]

Once the Rhine-Maidens have left, Hagen, Gunther and the other hunters arrive, afraid they had lost Siegfried. All prepare to halt — and Hagen, following his plan, asks Siegfried if it is true that he can understand birdsong. The hero says no: 'Since I've heard women singing, I've quite forgotten those songsters.'[33] Anyway, reminded of his youth, Siegfried offers to tell his story — which the others joyfully accept. Then Siegfried evokes his childhood with Mime, how he forged his sword, his fight against the dragon, his vengeance upon the Nibelung. Hagen then has him drink a memory-potion 'so that distant things don't escape you!'[34] Immediately, Siegfried recovers his memory! He remembers his first meeting with Brünnhilde and recounts it ecstatically — to general astonishment. Hagen takes the opportunity to strike Siegfried in the back with a spear. Then he flees before the anxious witnesses, declaring: 'A false oath I avenged.'[35] In the grip of woe, Gunther turns to Siegfried who, as he dies, evokes one more time, as if transfigured, his meeting with Brünnhilde and the kiss that woke her.

---

32   Ibid., p. 336. — Tr.
33   Ibid., p. 340. — Tr.
34   Ibid., p. 342. — Tr.
35   Ibid., p. 343. — Tr.

At nightfall, in the palace of the Gibichungen, Gutrune awaits the hunters' return. She is all the more worried at the sight of a woman, Brünnhilde surely, descending towards the Rhine. Suddenly, the dark call of Hagen's horn rings out. Hagen soon appears, announcing that Siegfried has been killed by a boar. Then Gunther arrives with the funeral cortège surrounding the hero's remains. Seeing that Siegfried was killed by a spear-blow, Gutrune, mad with sadness, accuses her brother of the murder. The king defends himself and puts the blame on Hagen, who does not hesitate to claim the slaying and the ring, making good on his 'sacred right of conquest' (*heiliges Beute-Recht hab' ich mir nun errungen*). Trying to protect his sister's 'inheritance,' Gunther tries to stop him.[36] Hagen kills him — but when he tries to take the ring, Siegfried's hand rises, to the horror of all witnesses. Then Brünnhilde arrives from the Rhine: she, true wife of Siegfried, whom grief has gifted the wisdom of Erda's daughters, would avenge the hero. Gutrune, learning the truth of Siegfried's first meeting with Brünnhilde, curses Hagen, who hatched the plot, and flings herself on her brother's body. Brünnhilde, long contemplates Siegfried's face, then, mastering her sadness, solemnly praises the courage and faithfulness of him who, like no other, respected every vow he made and who was obliged to betray them without ever wishing to do so. To the gods who condemned her and Siegfried to damnation, she sends two crows bearing the *desired* message: the end of the world is here — and the fire of the pyre where Siegfried's corpse burns is the same that will burn 'Valhalla's proud-standing stronghold.' Brünnhilde herself, mounted on her horse, flings herself on the pyre to be united with Siegfried 'in mightiest love' (*in mächtigster Minne*).[37] The fire overtakes the palace of the Gibichungen. Everything is coming unstuck; the Rhine's waters burst their banks and cover the earth. Hagen tries one last time to take the ring; but the Rhine-Maidens drag him with them into the depths of

---

36 Ibid., p. 346. — Tr.
37 Ibid., p. 350. — Tr.

the river. In the heavens, Valhalla burns. The flames surround Wotan and the other gods seated in the hall. All is finished.

Then from the orchestra-pit rises a *Leitmotiv* which we have only heard once so far, in *The Valkyrie* (III, 1), when Sieglinde, having learnt that she is carrying Siegmund's son, cries to Brünnhilde at the height of emotion: 'Sublimest wonder! Glorious maid! You true-hearted woman, I thank you for sacred solace! For him whom we loved I'll save what's most dear.'[38] This *Leitmotiv* is the hymn to life which renews itself, perpetuates itself the same in form but always different. In *The Twilight of the Gods*, following the intermingling of the *Motive* of the power of the gods and of the primordial waters, it is the musical symbol of *regeneration*, of the 'supreme mystery' that Wagner wanted to entrust to music alone and, at the same time, the evocation of the vision of the Edda, according to which three sons of Wotan, escaping the catastrophe of *Ragnarök*, recover the ancient 'tables of the gods' — and build a new world.

---

38   Ibid., p. 178. — Tr.

III

FIGURES

Although the author would go on to write a whole book showing how the superhumanist tendency and its 'new myth' originated, in fact, with Richard Wagner, and confuting repeated Nietzschean attempts to disguise the fact, Friedrich Nietzsche was the first to give explicit form in his works to the ideas common to both, and to their rich cultural, artistic and political inheritance. As such, he remains an indispensable reference for those who wish to take the same perspective. In this article, which appeared in *Nouvelle École*, no. 18 (May–June 1972), Locchi deals with the issue of Nietzsche's 'whitewashing' and the 'use' of Nietzsche by the hegemonic culture, in its infancy in those days, but which was already accompanied by attempts at 'rehabilitating' him for an improbable 'political correctness' *avant la lettre*. The treatment of this subject also offers an opportunity to remind ourselves of the essential points of the German philosopher, of whose thinking Locchi represents a direct continuation, on the basis of an intimate knowledge and a contemplation of the totality of Nietzsche's constantly renewed throughout his life, which few of our French contemporaries can claim.

1

Nietzsche and His 'Rehabilitators'

IT IS ALL OVER the papers in Paris. 'Three figures dominate the philosophical horizon today,' states *Combat* (4 May 1972): 'Marx, Freud, Nietzsche, whose influence colours all contemporary scholarship.' And since Nietzsche has been 'somewhat neglected' till now, it is he, above all, that we must 'revisit.' More precisely, as a *Figaro* columnist naïvely remarked in relation to a television programme dedicated to *Zarathustra*, we must *rehabilitate* Nietzsche.

To say that Nietzsche has been 'neglected' these last few years is pure euphemism. Official culture in post-War society has quite simply banished him, *put him on the Index*. Moreover, his story is rather familiar. The philosophers and ideologues of the Third Reich claimed Nietzsche and his work. They extolled National Socialism as the *movement* for which the visionary of Sils-Maria would have called. Better (or worse) still, many well-known authors, declared opponents of National Socialism, recognized the *validity* of these claims, or made only tentative objections. This was the case, to name a few, with Karl Löwith, celebrated author of *From Hegel to Nietzsche* (1941), and with György Lukács, who attempted to unmask 'the destruction of reason from Nietzsche to Hitler' (*Von Nietzsche zu Hitler* [Frankfurt: Fischer Bücherei, 1962], from Lukács, *Die Zerstörung der Vernunft* [Neuwied–Berlin: Hermann–Luchterhand, 1966]), and also with Fr. Valentini, S. J., who recognized the *Hakenkreuz* on the red-white-black flag as the symbol of eternity, becoming and the Eternal Return of the Identical.

So it was unavoidable that the Nuremberg moment should come for Nietzsche, as it had come for his *Sternenfreund* (star-friend) Richard Wagner. But that period is now over. Today, we are 'rehabilitating' Nietzsche, just as we are always 'rehabilitating' Wagner.

The main purpose of such a *rehabilitation*, which is not always explicit, is purely political. That is, to demonstrate the nonexistence of the filial bond between Nietzsche's works and the National Socialist enterprise, and that only a vulgar and abusive reading might lead one to detect a Nietzschean *heredity* in the Hitlerist movement. Clearly one cannot find National Socialism to have so 'noble' an origin as Nietzsche's thought. So then his 'rehabilitators'' hope, by means of a 'novel' but 'legitimate' *reading*, to make Nietzsche's work suitable for *integration* into the cultural patrimony of fashionable (democratic, socialist, even protest-oriented) ideologies.

All such efforts are utterly ridiculous. They tell either of a dazzling philosophical stupidity or of an authentic intellectual dishonesty.

One may of course (and perhaps it is inevitable that one will) wonder how Nietzsche would in fact have responded to a phenomenon like National Socialism. Moreover, there is no doubt that *on his own account*, if we take the trouble to *let him speak*, Nietzsche takes a stand as the *sworn* enemy of every movement that dominates society and 'culture' at the present time.

Nietzsche is not a philosopher like any other. Nor does he wish to be, and says so loudly. From now on, he declares, the philosopher's task is not limited to mere reflection on the past or the compartmentalization of knowledge. The philosopher must be an *artist* who takes man himself for his raw material. He must be the one to give mankind a goal and to compel him to seek the means to achieve it. Thus, Nietzsche announces the end of the old philosophy. He announces the birth of a thought free, at last, from the thrall of that 'Circe of the philosophers,' saved from *'moral' prejudice*.[1]

---

1   Nietzsche, *Daybreak*, Preface, 3. — Tr.

We have made Nietzsche a martyr of the 'search for truth'. A strange posthumous destiny, which he had foreseen, of course, and protested in advance. For the 'search for truth,' to which Nietzsche turned at a certain point in his speculation, consisted in the refutation and destruction of a *particular truth* which had been historically 'willed' and asserted by 'Christian morality': that is, 'slave-morality'. Furthermore, at the strictly gnoseological level, this 'search' completed the Kantian critique of Reason.

Kant had shown the impassable limits of Pure Reason. But, Nietzsche observed, he had immediately reasserted the rights of an *absolute*, recognizing the possibility of attaining 'the truth' and answering 'ultimate questions' through Practical Reason. In Nietzsche's eyes, this was to kill God only to fall in adoration before the *donkey who whinnies, 'Yea!'*[2] Nietzsche's speculation thereby takes a *critical* turn. Nietzsche undertakes to demonstrate the limits of Practical Reason. There can be no 'absolute truth': *true* and *false* are simply 'interested' *points of view*. All assertion is at once true *and* false; everything is *arbitrary*. Reason is but a *means*, an instrument. It is never the *principle*, the beginning of discourse or action. On the contrary, it *receives* this principle, which is an implicit *goal*. In short, its task is to clarify the way to the achievement of this goal and to reaffirm its principle in every circumstance and against every obstacle.

This *Irrationalismus*, this 'Destruction of Reason' with which the Marxist Lukács (followed by many others) charge Nietzsche, only appears as such when one *maintains* the perspective Nietzsche claims himself to have *historically surpassed*. In fact, Nietzsche simply puts Reason in its place. He thinks of it much as we, today, might think of an 'electronic brain': as a *logical machine* destined to serve us, which receives its information from us and can only provide answers contain potentially in the information received. For man is not the servant of abstract, universal and transcendent Reason. Reason, the faculty of

---

2 Nietzsche, *Zarathustra*, iv 'The Awakening.' — Tr.

logical thought and action, is the servant of man and man's will. In this sense, all assertions are arbitrary because they are all *human*; and every man expresses a *unique perspective* on the universe.

Nevertheless, man must assert and assert himself. Here, Nietzsche is the opposite of a *relativist* or *nihilist*. Had he fallen for the egalitarian illusion, he might have become one or the other: an *equivalence* between perspectives would fatally have led to anarchism and paralysis. But Nietzsche is a *superhumanist*. For him, one perspective is always worth more than another: it *must* be worth more than another. The destiny of all mankind is governed, at every historical 'moment,' by a broader, higher perspective which *encompasses* the others and *organizes* them hierarchically within itself. This is the perspective of the *superior man*. And only for as long as egalitarianism and levelling triumph, for as long as the *last man* lives can there be, in effect, *one single* perspective, one 'absolute truth.' But a *miserable* truth.

Nietzsche does not exclude the possibility. It could happen, he says. So we must *prevent* it. This is why Nietzsche also (and above all) wants his work to serve as a grand exercise in provocation and seduction, rousing, by 'poetic means,' a new type of man, a 'higher man,' eternally 'tending towards the Superman,' thereby assuring mankind's unending *historical becoming*, unending self-creation and self-recreation.

Nietzsche does not hide the 'immorality' of his project. But, just as all truth is *also* falsehood, he asserts that everything moral is *also* amoral. For him, life has only an *aesthetic* meaning. Hitherto, he writes, man has drawn his strength from the conviction that there exists an *ultimate goal* which would express the absolutely Good and True. From now on, he knows that 'God is dead'; that there is no ultimate goal. So all that remains for him is to assume the role he had till then assigned to God: to draw 'from the Earth,' and no longer 'from the Beyond,' the life-force he needs; to give his life a meaning and mankind a objective, in full knowledge that this objective, once achieved, will evanesce into nothing; that he must then redefine his meaning, once again, and find another objective. A myth of Sisyphus? No. for Sisyphus *did not will* his travail: he was *compelled* by a malignant God. A mere *victim*, he did not *direct* himself; his action was *directed*.

To Nietzsche, Sisyphus represents 'the frightful rule of folly and chance which has hitherto gone by the name of "history" (the folly of the "greatest number" is only its last form).'³ He is, if you prefer, the hero-victim of Fortune, to whom he gives the name of God, or universal suffrage, or the moral primacy of the proletariat. The true hero for whom Nietzsche calls is Sisyphus' antithesis. He is one who consciously refuses to be *simultaneously* his own victim and torturer; who is capable of willing 'his own fall that the Superman might be.'

> To teach man the future of humanity as his will, as dependent on a man's will, and to prepare for great exploits and comprehensive attempts at discipline and cultivation [...] that a new type of philosopher and commander will at some point be necessary, at the sight of which all hidden, fearsome, and benevolent spirits on earth may well look pale and dwarfish.

Therefore, in its basic outlines, Nietzsche's *project*, which he sometimes calls his 'great politics' of the future, is perfectly clear and not susceptible to any equivocation. Nietzsche never tires of specifying what he opposes and what he favours. He declares open war on *egalitarianism* in all its historic guises (which he lumps together, anyhow, with disdain): against Christianity, which, with the formula of all men's equality before God, infected the Graeco-Roman world with egalitarian dogma; against the 'liberalism' expressed by the Revolution of 1789; against democracy and the 'tyranny of universal suffrage'; against socialism, communism, anarchism, *etc.*

Observing his own times, Nietzsche already sees all these forms of egalitarianism *converging* upon a more or less conscious nihilism and the 'democratization of souls' resulting, in Europe, in the formation of an immense 'mass of slaves.' He foresees the amalgamation and levelling of European peoples. He even surmises that economic imperatives will impel the movement towards European unification. He takes this

---

3   *Beyond Good and Evil*, v, 203.

'party of peace,' this 'movement of last men,' to be a practically irreversible event which nihilism will only aggravate. Nietzsche does not intend to oppose this process of 'massification.' On the contrary, he advises 'his own' to *accelerate* it. But he mentions another movement, 'his movement,' which he sees taking shape and gaining strength. This movement is the 'party of war.' A day will come, he says, when the 'race of masters,' the 'caste of lords' of which this party is the means if *expression*, will make the *mass* its own *tool*, thereby giving it a *meaning*, and will establish a 'government of the Earth' (from Europe) over a world globalized by technological progress.

We need not describe or dissect the Nietzschean project further. To ignore it, or to deny it, one must not have read Nietzsche (or claim that Nietzsche thought the opposite of what he wrote, which is not unheard of). In the last analysis, it is a resolutely *anti-egalitarian* project which opposes egalitarianism in all of its most recent guises.[4]

Given these facts, it will strike any opponent of egalitarianism as most unlikely that Nietzsche's work should be 'rehabilitated.' Nevertheless, Nietzsche's *natural* enemies have always tried to press him into service of their schemes, and nowadays more then ever. We might therefore wonder how such a manoeuvre is imaginable, how it might be carried out and, above all, given the dangers 'egalitarians' face in 'handling' the Nietzschean project, what its reasons might be.

This last question is certainly easiest to answer. If fashionable ideologues feel *compelled* to *try* to 'rehabilitate' Nietzsche, it is because they cannot keep him from *speaking*. Nietzsche's work is there, *provoking* and *seducing* despite the anathemas. Besides, like some monstrous ruminant, our *civilization* cannot keep itself off the most dangerous narcotics and stimulants; it can hope at best to *mithridatize* itself against them. So the egalitarian world tries to *scramble* this disturbing

---

[4] Nietzsche even foresaw these 'challenges' and gave a striking description. The terms in which the last man expresses his desires in *Thus Spake Zarathustra* anticipates, in a rather grotesquely register, the conclusions of Marcuse's 'utopian' speculation.

and disquieting voice with its own noise. It tries to put a distorting lens (which it calls 'clarifying') between the work ('difficult to read') and the myopic reader. Thus, it *falsifies*.

These methods are not new. One of them, the most time-honoured, is the imposition of a *chronological* division onto Nietzsche's work. There is supposed to have been a period of *immaturity*, the Romantic and Wagnerian Nietzsche; then a period of *maturity*, considered pre-eminently 'valuable';[5] and, finally, a third period in which his thought was influenced by madness, as yet subterranean, but still active (and in which what we know to be his *project* was definitively formulated). In which case it would be best not to take seriously the 'extravagances' of the last period, lest they contradict the 'authentic' thought of the 'still healthy' philosopher.[6]

This critique has the advantage of depending upon an analysis that *traces back* to the author himself. But it is concerned only with the *objects* of Nietzsche's speculation. It tells us nothing *about the speculation itself*. In truth, Nietzsche always *sought the same thing* from the beginning of his activity. He noted it himself, and not without pride, when he gave his early works new prefaces a little before sinking into madness. There is certainly an evolution through Nietzsche's work; but this evolution is simply the ever more complete *grasping* of the *will* that moves him and, thereby, of all that opposes this will, and of the means it must employ. The 'revaluation of all values' is already proposed implicitly, we might say 'instinctually', in *The Birth of Tragedy*: the Wagnerian Nietzsche who invokes the appearance of Siegfried is

---

[5] It is symptomatic of all Nietzsche's 'rehabilitators' to rate this second, the period of *Human, All Too Human* — in which Nietzsche himself expressly stated his wish to compel himself, out of intellectual honesty and in order to 'sharpen' his senses, to 'think against himself' — higher than the rest.

[6] Catholic critics were the first to develop this argument, insisting on the general 'morbidity' of a work whose author is said to have been afflicted from his earliest youth by a hypothetical illness (which diagnosticians of his era wished to consider syphilitic).

already the Nietzsche who heralds the higher man and the 'race of masters' and who tells, to this end, the myth of the Eternal Return.

Another method of 'rehabilitation' with innumerable variations[7] is the claim that Nietzsche's work (presented for the occasion as 'fragmentary,' 'discontinuous,' 'aphoristic,' *etc.*) hides its 'true meaning' behind a veil of signs, 'ciphers,' 'metaphors,' so the appearance of argument destroys itself in step with its own development. This is of the same kind as the *scrambling* method: if the evidence does not fit, it must be *something else*. This is what is 'demonstrated' by loudly ignoring the emperor's nudity.

In fact, to those *with eyes to see*, this stratagem only reveals a *constitutional incapacity to assimilate* Nietzsche's text. Still more, it attests to the *need* of a certain *type* of reader to ignore the truth of a text he feels, perhaps mistakenly, will offend and *humiliate* him in his deepest being. One cannot even blame the difficulties of reading and comprehending the argument. Certainly, in a book like *Thus Spake Zarathustra*, Nietzsche forms his material into a *myth* in order to shatter the 'rationality' of his era's philosophical jargon, which is none other than the rationality of the egalitarian discourse imposed by secular history. But, in his last works above all, he also provided the *keys* to the authentic interpretation of the myth. Moreover, he *explicated* the nature and genesis of this myth which he conceived consciously as a 'doctrine which, in unleashing the deadliest pessimism, will secure the selection of the strongest element,' and 'which will make humanity to perish, save those who can bear it.'

Confronted by Nietzsche's work, a man who still believes in absolute Good and Truth will not, *cannot* accept the soundness of an argument belonging to a new dimension of historical consciousness. He passes through this dimension and shuts himself off to it. Thus, the revolutionary proof that Nietzsche develops remains inaccessible

---

[7] Let us cite just two recent examples: Jean-Michel Rey, *L'enjeu des signes: lecture de Nietzsche* (Seuil, 1971); Sarah Kaufmann, *Nietzsche et la métaphore* (Payot, 1972).

to enemies of his *project*, though it does allow them to access its background, which fascinates them endlessly, and which ought to lose them. This background is the philosophical (thus *critical*) aspect of the work, completing the speculation of Immanuel Kant in its own way. The 'invisible proof,' this 'garden which the *Others* cannot enter,' is the entire work in its 'poetry,' that is, in its simultaneous presentation of a myth, a *psychologically active* argument (creating a new type of man), the outline of a project of 'great politics' and the preparation of the means necessary for its realization.

The fascination the *critical* aspects of Nietzsche's work exercises upon the Christian, egalitarian world es explained without difficulty, but slightly differently. This critique (Nietzsche states explicitly) represents, in fact, the *historical continuation* of Christian, egalitarian speculation: it begins with the *final* Christian, egalitarian perspective. Goethe said that, to destroy an 'idea,' one need only 'think it through to its end.' In his 'second period,' Nietzsche took it upon himself to think the egalitarian idea, the Christian morality of Good and Evil, *through to its end, destroying* it by pushing it to the point *at which is falls into its opposite*.

Hannah Arendt reproached Nietzsche, along with Marx and Freud, for having relapsed into *illusion*, having 'destroyed tradition.' This is a novel error. Unlike Kant, Marx or Freud, Nietzsche does not claim to have found the *true* answers to ultimate questions. On the contrary, and magisterially, he gives his own answers to his own questions. Against the arbitrariness of the type of man that dominates his time, whom he scorns, he sets his own *arbitrariness* and his own *Geschmack* (his own taste). The myth he proposes is not (nor does it try to be) anything other than a *work of art*: it aims to seduce, to provoke. Everyday language naïvely calls this work a propaganda-campaign. Nietzsche, under the mask of Zarathustra, becomes a preacher.

It is worth noting that Nietzsche, all his life, never tired of comparing himself to Socrates, on the one hand, and Jesus of Nazareth, on the other. In his work, Socrates is presented as the philosopher whose dialectical reflection opened the doors of the pagan world to the egalitarian virus, surreptitiously depriving this world of its means of defence. Jesus, along with Paul of Tarsus, slipping through this open door, infected the pagan world with the egalitarian *disease*. Nietzsche presents himself as what, to the egalitarian world, Socrates and Jesus were, together, to the pagan world. Whence the double aspect of his work: *critical* and *destructive* when he plays the part of Socrates; *poetic* and *mythmaking* when he plays the part of Jesus.

It is quite natural that proponents of the Christian, egalitarian enterprise should feel the need to *make use* of Nietzschean critique and feel increasingly that they cannot do without it. Nietzsche, let us repeat, *thought their world through to its end*. And so they have much to learn from him about themselves. Similarly, at the more down-to-earth level of everyday propaganda, it is just as easy to see why they redouble their efforts to efface any trace of 'kinship' between this endlessly fascinating philosophy and the National Socialist phenomenon. But since this 'kinship' is undeniable, one had better acknowledge it.

However, it does not allow us to make *any meaningful argument* either against Nietzsche or in favour of National Socialism.

In fact, to approach such a problem with any consistency, we must begin by asking what we understand by the word 'kinship' in discourse of this sort. One might reasonably argue that Paul of Tarsus *falsified* Christ's preaching, or that Christ would not have been 'recognized' by the Paul's 'Christianity' (any more than Marx by the 'Marxism' of Lenin, Trotsky or Mao Zedong). But as interesting as such an assertion might be intellectually, it would be *historically insignificant*. In reality, the strength and greatness of the Gospel consists precisely in its having historically engendered all Christianities, and its continuing, no less historically, to *reabsorb* them back into itself. Any similar 'reading' of Nietzsche, any *interpretation* (including that of the Hitlerist movement) may be judged and dismissed as *improper*.

But a judgement of this sort, however well founded, has no real significance. It resorts to pure abstraction, that kingdom of the absolute within whose bounds there can be no 'communication.' Because what counts from the historical perspective is not whether Paul of Tarsus did or did not *betray* the words of Christ. It is the fact that he *claimed* Him and that he was *heard* only inasmuch as he claimed Him. The same goes for Lenin and Trotsky in relation to Marx. The genius of the founder of a religion, an intellectual influence or the founder of a school is measured by the abundance of 'products' which situate themselves *within his discourse* and even claim to *be that discourse*. There have been a multitude of Christian sects, each one of which may have realized an *aspect* of the *project* proposed by Christ, but of which only a few have gained the *historical weight* necessary to determine what Christianity *actually is*: that is, who Christ *is becoming in posterity*.[8]

Like Christ, Nietzsche claims to be the initiator of a historical movement. This movement has engendered tendencies and schools which may *objectively* have betrayed him, but which, from the strictly *historical* perspective, all appear as his *reality* and *continuation*. This must be taken into account by any who wish to speak with even a little coherence of the relationship between Nietzsche and National Socialism. In his *Konservative Revolution in Deutschland*, Armin Mohler gathered the profusion of philosophical, political and literary *sects* of the inter-War period who claimed the Nietzschean myth. These interrelated sects issued verdicts upon one another in the fashion of Marxist sects. Regarding National Socialism, they adopted rather different attitudes. Therefore, if it is true that National Socialism was 'Nietzschean' in the sense that it situated itself within the anti-egalitarian discourse whose contours Nietzsche helped to define, it is nonetheless false that all 'Nietzscheanism' is National Socialist. Just as 'leftist aberrations' do not compromise Marx in the eyes of orthodox communists, National Socialism does not in the least 'compromise' the Nietzschean *project*.

---

8   Besides, what would it matter is these developments worked historically 'in spite of Him'? It would simply show that Christ knew not what He did as He did it.

This text dates from January 1969, and appeared in *Nouvelle École*, no. 13, on the occasion of the French translation of Oswald Spengler's *Der Mensch und die Technik* ('Man and Technics'). Indeed, the author's 'untimely' meditations remain durably interesting in one respect thanks to a postmodern and superhumanist reinterpretation of the work of Spengler, still too often limited to the role of a 'thinker of Decline,' and, in another respect, in connection to more general questions regarding the times in which we live, with what the exposition of 'originary thinking' might tell us about the choice that faces us.

2

Regarding *Man and Technics*

Untimely Meditations on Oswald Spengler's Late Works

THERE ARE REVELATORY signs. By attempting to force a 'reading' of Marx upon so-called *avant-garde* thought, Louis Althusser (*Pour Marx*, Maspero) is winding the clock backwards without realizing it. In fact, the religion of progress is entangled, in its deepest being, with the will to stop history at a 'final moment'. And from his point of view, Althusser is right: Marx is effectively the culmination — at least, he initiates the culmination — of the Western egalitarian thought founded by Christianity. Therefore, precisely inasmuch as modern man declares himself, in the majority, egalitarian, 'modern' thought is condemned to perpetual *rumination* on Marx; and our societies are condemned to rerun through the rigours of the nineteenth century, and especially the German nineteenth century, in a sort of tragicomic game.

However, the last century has also bequeathed us a thinking which stands *beyond* Marx, *beyond* egalitarianism's bimillenary discourse. The philosophical work of Friedrich Nietzsche and the artistic and metapolitical work of Richard Wagner have inaugurated this *new* thinking, the only thought that can be called revolutionary, since it represents, within a cyclical view of history, the *return* of an origin which had been completely forgotten, therefore lost and, consequently, never *given*, but also, within a linear view, an *overcoming*, an opening into an unknown, exhilarating destiny.

This thought, as *Urdenken*, originary thought, expresses itself in forms proper to *myth* and, in its historical youth, as generatrix of myths, invites genuine creation, incites us to consciously accept the possibility of man's transformation. These days, since it is non-egalitarian, anti-egalitarian, it is denounced or, wherever possible, abandoned to falsification and improper interpretation. But it is clear that our age cannot keep to Marx, to the mere repetition of a defunct instant, and that it seeks to return, more or less consciously, to the 'opening' to be found in the thought of Nietzsche and Wagner. So one should not be unduly surprised by the publication of a French translation of Oswald Spengler's *Man and Technics* by a publisher (Gallimard) and in a series (*Idées*) which have hitherto been the vehicles for quite different currents of thought.

A blurb on the cover draws the reader's attention, among other things, to the fact that Spengler 'tried to demonstrate that the privileges enjoyed by Whites will be seized from them by the peoples of the Third World, for whom technology will become a weapon against Western civilization.' *Quos deus vult perdere...*[1] Spengler, a pessimist, does indeed assert that Western civilization of *fatally* condemned. But he does not incite us to renunciation, to passive acceptance of a purportedly inevitable dispossession, but, quite to the contrary, to stand firm 'like that Roman soldier whose bones were found in front of a door in Pompeii, who, during the eruption of Vesuvius, died at his post because they forgot to release him.'[2]

---

[1] Latin expression after a fragment of Euripedes: '*Quos Deus vult perdere, pruis dementat*' ('He whom God would destroy He first makes mad'). — Ed.

[2] *Man and Technics*, transl. C. F. Atkinson (Budapest: Legend Books, 2023), p. 77. — Tr.

Those Who Bear the Burden of Decline

As *mythic* thinking, the importance of Spengler's work is to be found not in the direct statements on which he imposes the logical, necessarily logical, form of his discourse, but in his position towards history, in the value-judgements that underpin his vision. This is not to say that his prophecy is false. On the contrary, the *moment at which he speaks* remains irremediable susceptible to the *decline of the West*. But the attitude he presents, which involves the heroic sacrifice of what is 'Western' in us, is also the *guarantee* of a new dawn of what in us is already beyond the 'egalitarian West.'

Spengler himself never forgets that his thought takes place entirely within a Nietzschean framework, aiming simply to respond to the *Fragestellung*, to the problem as outlined by Nietzsche. One must keep in view that, within this framework and approaching this problem, and in conformity to his 'Prussian' temperament, Spengler only assumes, and only tries to assume, the limited perspective of the moment at which he lives: that is, the first three decades of the twentieth century, which, in Nietzsche's millenary vision, represent nothing other than the onset of *European nihilism*, which contains the condition *sine qua non* of the transformation of man into superman. Nietzsche wrote: 'I love him who liveth in order to know, and seeketh to know in order that the Superman may hereafter live. Thus seeketh he his own downgoing (*Untergang*).'[3] Spengler consciously desired to be one of those men who bear the burden decline.

In Spengler's lifework, *Man and Technics* represents the beginning of the culmination of his thinking. This culmination is very little known, since it remains in a state of sketch and fragment, published in two volumes since 1966 by C. H. Beck (*Urfragen*: 'Questions of Origin'; *Frühzeit der Weltgeschichte*: Early Days of World History[4]). On

---

3 *Thus Spake Zarathustra*, Prologue, 4. — Tr.
4 *Early Days of World History*, transl. Constantin von Hoffmeister (Budapest: Legend Books, 2022).

first sight, the vision Spengler develops in *Man and Technics* might surprise those who know him only through his *Decline of the West*. It is a 'universal' vision, apparently at odds with his anti-universalist vision in the *Decline*, where many specific histories are presented, each the product of a very specific *Hochkultur* ('high culture'), the expression of a type of man constituting, so to speak, a distinct species. But this contradiction is only apparent. Spengler clearly encompasses the first vision within the second, the incompleteness of this prospective *encompassing* due simply to the incompleteness of the work as a whole.

Two Characterizations

For the 'second' Spengler, mankind has undergone four great 'transformations' since his origin. His history is therefore composed of four essential *moments*: *a, b, c, d*. But Spengler does not always express his thoughts very clearly; and these four moments sometimes seem to reduce to just three. That is the case in *Man and Technics*, which we now know (since the posthumous publications by C. H. Beck) to constitute the first sketch of a developing thought.

In his *Provisions for the 'Urfragen,'* Spengler characterizes the four fundamental moments of history as follows:

(*a*) Liberation from the constraints of the species; the emergence of races; the formation of the human type; the emergence of consciousness (*Bewusstwerdung*);

(*b*) Low-density crystallizations of population in local complexes from 15,000 B.C.; *cultural* barycentres with their own well-defined spheres of influence;

(*c*) 'Specific cultures' (*Einzelkulturen*: Spengler distinguishes and opposes the terms *Kultur* and *Zivilisation*) diffused across a world that man has totally saturated; 'amoebas' of organic structure from 5,000 B.C.;

(*d*) *Hochkulturen* ('high cultures') with 'lifespans' (*Lebensläufe*) fully formed around 3,000 B.C.; transformation of dynamic *cultures* into fixed *civilizations* ('the fellahin as ruins').

This division succeeds the tripartite division found in *Man and Technics*, which we might summarize as follows:

(1) The birth of man; hand and tool; *Schauen und Ahnen* (a formula we might translate as 'capacity for anticipation, for divinatory vision');

(2) Language and *enterprise*, the latter denoting 'concerted collective action'; *Sprechen und Denken*, speech and thought;

(3) The end times: the advent and dissolution of mechanized culture.

It is difficult to relate these two characterizations to one another. At a glance, they seem to overlap: moment 1 corresponds, more or less, to moments *a* and *b*, moment 2 to phase *c* and to the *Hochkulturen* of phase *d* (see *The Decline of the West*), moment 3 overlapping only with the final phase (*civilization*) of Western *Faustian culture*. But then, the correspondence is not perfect: for each comes from a different perspective. All this is of secondary importance in relation to the essential: the resolutely anti-egalitarian objective of Spengler's work.

This is why it is entirely pointless to dilate upon certain notions inherited from the 'scientific language' of the time of writing. For example, that Spengler related 'hominization' to the emergence of the hand–tool binomial tells us nothing of his *conception of man*. We must therefore turn our attention elsewhere, to where the author explicitly places the *value* of the human as opposed to the nonhuman. Now, Spengler is very clear and very Nietzschean on this point. Man, he affirms, is a 'beast of prey,' but an animal *sui generis, generis unici*: for he is the only one to 'break the constraints of the species.'

Man appears as such when, alongside 'a species-instinct always to perpetuate himself in full force,' 'reflexive thought and action detach themselves and assert their autonomy in relation to the species.' Every man (dealing here with creator-man) is a species unto himself. The soul of original man 'is deeper and more passionate than that of any other animal'; it 'confines itself to an intransigently oppositional attitude towards the rest of the world, whose own creative power has excluded him.'

Spengler adds:

> This soul moves ceaselessly onwards in ever-wider separation from *all* nature. The weapons of beasts of prey are natural; but man's fist, armed with his artificially fabricated, imagined and selected weapon, is not. Here begins *art* as the concept antinomic to *nature*. Here also begins the tragedy of man: for of these two, nature is the stronger... The struggle against nature is hopeless; and yet, it must be fought to its end.

Man Against Nature

It follows clearly from the above that, for Spengler, *history* is based upon man's revolt against nature, a revolt already encapsulated in his breaking of the *constraints of the species*. This claim is fundamental. On the other hand, one might, and one ought to find Spengler's explanation of the *cause* of the break (the emergence of the hand–tool binomial) wanting, an attitude all the more justified given that Spengler was the first to dispute his own 'explanation,' often considering it just *one* cause among others or the necessary but not insufficient material condition of humanization.

In fact, as his posthumous writings reveal, until his death, Spengler was preoccupied by the question of man's origin, by that 'first moment,' which he succeeded in *divining* by means of the dazzling intuition of his poetic genius, but which always escaped his philosophical striving. In *Man and Technics*, the description of this 'first moment' remains vague. Spengler speaks of the soul of this first, 'solitary' man who broke from the constraints of the species, but without ever specifying the concrete forms of this break; he asserts the 'total opposition' of man and nature without ever indicating in relation to *which nature* the original man defined himself concretely in his action, the *concrete object* of his struggle and his domination.

To our eyes, this shortcoming unconsciously was unconsciously *willed* by Spengler himself, since that allowed him to curtail his *tragic* vision of history, to 'hold firm' to the limited present that he totally assumes. The inevitable consequence is that the elements of his *definition of the human*, rather than all being situated at the *moment* of history's beginning, are distributed across all the phases outlined above. For it is quite true that man's revolt against nature must be catastrophic. But if this revolt is to be found in its entirety at the first *moment* of history, from the 'first historical act,' then man's tragic destiny must also be fount in its entirety at every moment, as if borne by a *will to history* endlessly asserted, endlessly declared by the same gesture throughout the epic of creation and in the final catastrophe inscribed logically into the realization of the goal.

If, on the other hand, the catastrophe is not present from the *first moment*, it becomes the property of a *final moment* and history follows a parabola to a final tragedy. Spengler *wills* mankind's tragic destiny; but with an immense, Promethean pride, he claims the experience and passion of this tragedy *for his civilization alone*: that is, for Faustian man; for the 'Vikings of the spirit.' He gives this opinion implicitly, perhaps without catching himself, in a passage whose contradictions and *omissions* are full of significance.

He writes:

> Faustian culture, the culture of the West is probably not the last but is certainly the most powerful, the most vehement and, in the interior conflict between its comprehensive intellectuality and its lack of spiritual harmony, all the more tragic. It is conceivable that some latecomer might succeed it in the next millennium (a culture might come to light somewhere on the plains between the Vistula and the Amur). But it is here, *in our culture and in ourselves*, that the combat between nature and man (whose historical destiny has led him to pit himself against her) is concluded, once and for all.

The contradiction is clear. If man's historical destiny is completed by his revolt against nature, and if this revolt is completed by our Faustian culture, then history as a whole also ends with us. Who, then, could this 'latecomer' be, this culture 'between the Vistula and the Amur,' if not man's *return to nature*, his relapse into the constraints of the species — that is, his *re-animalization*? A history after history is no longer history.

Let us return to the second *moment* described in *Man and Technics* in order to discern the elements belonging by right, *contra* Spengler, to the original definition of man. The first is 'language,' which emerged with what we now call the 'Neolithic Revolution.' For Spengler, if the *solitary* man of the first *moment* availed himself of words and gestures, he did not yet possess a language in the strict sense (grammar and syntax). In fact, language appears only to the extent that it is objectively imposed by 'concerted collective action' (*enterprise*), the first expressions of which were agriculture and the rearing of livestock. Here, as before, let us not discuss this 'provisional' assertion, but turn, instead, to the way Spengler perceives this constitutive element.

The Problem of Alienation

Within enterprise, Spengler makes a basic distinction between 'creation–planning' and 'execution'; between *born creators*, who are sole heirs to the *solitary men* of the preceding moment, and the executors; between *leaders* and *followers*. Citing Goethe's *Faust*, he even indicates that, in his view, the led are nothing but *tools* of the *thinking hand* of born creators:

> When to my car
> My money yokes six spankers, are
> Their limbs not my limbs? Is't not I
> On the proud racecourse that dash by?
> Mine all the forces I combine,

The four-and-twenty legs are mine![5]

Thus, man domesticates nature; but creator-man also domesticates follower-man, who is a *piece of nature*. Here we find Nietzsche's distinction between *Herrenmenschen* and 'slaves,' but with one crucial detail: the 'slave' does not amount to a true man, to a *historical* man, but to *nature*, at once instrument and object of the creator's enterprise. The *problem of alienation* which so torments Freudians and Marxists is here clarified in such a way as to permit, perhaps, a solution: alienation is the necessary counterpart of the expansion of the 'creator,' the beast of prey who breaks the constraints of the species, organizing and appropriating follower-men, part of nature, as his tools and instruments, but also as parts of his *body*. *Only the man who expresses himself in creation can be free*. Alienation never bothers the true man, but only the man who *remains in nature*, powerless to break out, nothing more than one among countless species. The historical fact par excellence is not alienation but the opposite of alienation: the *appropriation of all nature*, including human nature, by creator-man.

Not considering the binomials *language–enterprise* and *leaders–followers* to be original elements, Spengler associates the advent of the machine with the decline of the creator-men. Indeed, the creators only ever saw technology as a mere means. They always willed the *effort of creation* more than the *benefits of creation*: the hunt more than the prey. But once the machine was created, it paralyzed creative inspiration. 'Faustian thinking begins to feel sick with machines'; 'a weariness spreads; a sort of pacifism in the struggle against nature' becomes universal: 'the *flight of the born leaders* from the machine begins.'

In parallel, followers 'mutiny against their destiny, against the machine, against *standardized* life, against everything and against nothing.' An era of *masses* begins; 'but the mass is merely a negative residuum' — specifically the negation of the concept of organization — 'and

---

5   *The First Part of Goethe's Faust*, tr. John Anster (London: Routledge, 1887), p. 103. — Tr.

not viable on its own merit.' 'An army without officers is nothing but a horde of men, disarrayed and useless.' Moreover, the white man committed 'technological treason' when he handed technology to peoples of colour. The latter are bound to use it as a weapon against the former, and then to let it run to ruin.

Set alongside our own time, the exactitude of Spengler's *prediction* is impressive, even to the detail. Like Nietzsche's predictions, it humiliates the 'scientific' but invariably false prophecies of a Karl Marx. However, Spengler does not know, *does not wish to know*, whence his powers of foresight come. This leads him to see the cause of the decline of the West, and, by the same token, of historical man as a whole, in the machine. Even making allowances for the time of the text's composition, we cannot accept this point of view.

Western civilization is doomed not by technological progress but because the egalitarian utopia that inspired it for two thousand years has come into conflict with the exigencies of modern society. European man, committed to his utopia, is no longer in a position to assume the destiny of the world, to be the 'creator' of a new future. But it is also in Europe, and only in Europe, that a new transformation remains possible, that the refusal of egalitarianism and the *return to the species* can be asserted, and can be asserted again, *beyond* what two millennia of spiritual 'decadence' called 'Good' and 'Evil.' Spengler's thought is one assertion of this refusal.

'Prussian Socialism'

It is not uninteresting to recall here what attitude Spengler took towards Hitlerist National Socialism. He was frankly hostile, sometimes venomous, even if this hostility arose *within* an anti-egalitarian dialectic (in his *Konservative Revolution*, Armin Mohler counts Spengler among the 'Trotskyists of National Socialism'). In the posthumous writings of the author of the *Decline*, there are frequent allusions to the 'stupidity' of certain National Socialist ideas. he mocks their conception of *race*, emphasizing, against the professions of the NSDAP, that 'race is always bound up in selection, in the elite,' and that it is therefore 'a factor of class,' not of people.

His objections were those of a *social aristocrat*, a partisan of 'Prussian socialism,' who saw in National Socialism a 'democratic' and plebeian mass-movement. Here he follows other representatives of the *Konservative Revolution*, for whom the 'anti-egalitarian revolution' must necessarily be the work of an isolated elite, resolutely distant from the masses, and who violently upbraided Hitler for putting himself at the service of the plebs, when, in the aftermath of the tragic events of 1924, he decided, by means of the NSDAP, to make the masses his *tool*.

The following text appeared in 1973 in *Nouvelle École*, no. 23, as a review of Armin Mohler's famous essay, twenty-three years before its translation into French in 1993; but its interest is far greater than that of the book it takes as its subject. Two somewhat symmetrical aspects are worth highlighting, as Locchi did himself. On the one hand, the range and the importance of both of the phenomena — the movements and authors — Mohler considers and of the new sensibility underlying them. On the other, the transparently instrumental nature of the efforts to impute a basic unity to the *Konservative Revolution* extending even to its most disparate and marginal tendencies, and, inversely, its radical extraneity with respect to the rest of the German and European superhumanist panorama of the era, and in particular with respect to its most 'burdensome' political expressions.

3

Armin Mohler and the Conservative Revolution

BETWEEN 1918 and 1933, German cultural and political life was shaped by a powerful spiritual movement which declared itself determined "to clear away the ruins of the nineteenth century and to establish a new order of life." This movement took form, with more or less vigour, across almost all of Europe; but it was in Germany that it marked every domain of life and society most profoundly. It has been named the *Konservative Revolution*, the 'conservative revolution.' This 'metapolitical' phenomenon has been examined many times (and all too often by its enemies and on the basis of preconceived notions); but all in all, despite its fundamental historical importance, we still understand it quite poorly. In 1950, Dr. Armin Mohler aimed to fill in this lacuna by publishing his doctoral thesis, which he had defended the previous year at the University of Basle under the supervision of Professors Karl Jaspers and Herman Schmalenbach. This successful publication would be reedited into a veritable handbook and augmented by an imposing bibliography of nearly four hundred pages, which suffices to demonstrate the importance and richness of the writers of the *Konservative Revolution*.

A Thousand Directions

The task Armin Mohler took on was extremely arduous. Between 1918 and 1933, the *Konservative Revolution* never presented one unified aspect, one sole visage. Groping after a path of is own, it proliferated in a thousand apparently divergent directions, investing as much in art as in philosophy, in literature as in politics. Therefore, the *Konservative Revolution* formed a universe of its own whose depth and breadth may amaze those who come to it for the first time. Men as diverse as the 'first' Thomas Mann (exiled in 1933), Ernst Jünger and his brother Friedrich Georg, Oswald Spengler (*The Decline of the West*) Ernst von Salomon (*The Outlaws*), Alfred Baeumler (who became some sort of official academic philosopher of National Socialism), Stefan George and Hugo von Hofmannsthal, the jurist Carl Schmitt, the biologist Jacob von Uexküll, the anthropologist Hans F. K. Günther, the economist Werner Sombart, the archaeologist Gustaf Kossinna, Erwin Guido Kolbenheyer and Hans Grimm, Hans Blüher and Gottfried Benn, Ernst Wiechert and Rainer Maria Rilke, Max Scheler and Ludwig Klages, to just a few of the most famous: all were men of the *Konservative Revolution*. The works of these men instigated and animated, in ever-renewed impulses, a host of schools of thought and 'circles of friends,' secret and semi-secret organizations of an esoteric sort, literary cenacles, political parties and 'groupuscules,' associations aligned with the *Freikorps*, with the 'underground'[1] (already!), and of the most diverse orientations and around the most diversely articulated concerns and intentions.

These currents' kinship is apparent; though their shared mentality can be apprehended only with difficulty as long as one adopts a perspective exterior to the movement. On the other hand, the sense they all had of this ideological kinship did not keep them from nurturing enmities and fierce hatreds among themselves (more against those condemned as 'traitors' than against enemies). So it was that Walther

---

1 English in the original. — Tr.

Rathenau, whose works belong to the margins of the *Konservative Revolution*, was assassinated by terrorists who were no less "conservative-revolutionary." This affair is well-known from Salomon's account of it in *Die Geächteten* (The Outlaws).

Finally, as the author affirms in the preface, its 'spiritual proximity' to National Socialism wrongfully compromises the *Konservative Revolution* and risks skewing any analysis by casting a shadow over the facts of the matter. While recognising that this problem is all but insurmountable, Dr. Mohler tried to avoid the difficulties attendant on this uncomfortable proximity by bracketing the whole National Socialist phenomenon, whose historical destiny represents a distinct question, a 'lack of distance' from which still precludes an analysis today. He does remark, though, that the National Socialists, once they had come to power, made a priority of attacking certain representatives of the *Konservative Revolution* who refused to join. The 'Night of the Long Knives,' to cite only one event, settles scores not only between wings of the National Socialist movement but also between the Nazis and conservative-revolutionary 'Trotskyists.'

'Trotskyists'

'From a formal point of view,' writes Dr. Mohler,

> participants in the *Konservative Revolution* might be understood as the Trotskyists of National Socialism. Here, as in any great revolutionary movement, including communism, we find a large mass-party of uniform weight, on the one hand, and a myriad of little circles, on the other, distinguished by an intense intellectual life, exerting only a weak influence on the masses and, in terms of party-formation, managing at most to provoke marginal splits in the larger party, indulging in the organization of explosive sects and little elitist, barely coherent groups. When the larger party goes bankrupt, then comes the hour of the Trotskyist heresies.

We should note, in this connection, that, in fact, the *Konservative Revolution* underwent the inverse process, and that it was the serial bankruptcy of the little 'Trotskyist' sects that cleared National Socialism's path to power. But from Armin Mohler's perspective, this is of secondary importance, since his purpose is not to analyse a revolutionary machine but to sketch, as he states, a typology of the *Konservative Revolution*.

'Guiding Images'

Having noted that the origins of the *Konservative Revolution* date around the midpoint of the nineteenth century, Armin Mohler then tries to recover and describe what he calls the *Leitbilder*, the 'guiding ideas' (or, better, 'images') shared by all the writers of the *Konservative Revolution*.

He situates the origin of the 'world-image' (*Weltbild*) of the *Konservative Revolution* in the work of Friedrich Nietzsche: the Nietzsche of *Zarathustra* above all, but also the Nietzsche of *The Will to Power* and the *Genealogy of Morals*. Indeed, every *Leitbild* he adduces springs from Nietzsche's vision. One of these 'leading ideas' is without a doubt fundamental. This is the 'spherical' conception of history, as opposed to the *linear* conception shared, among others, by Marxism and Christianity. For the participants in the *Konservative Revolution*, history is not an infinite and indefinite progression. It is an *eternal return*. Mohler rightly emphasizes that this eternal return is best expressed not by the circle but by the *sphere* (*Kugel*), which 'means, to the *conservative-revolutionary* eye, that everything is contained in every moment; that present, past and future *coincide*.' He cites Nietzsche:

> Everything goeth, everything returneth; eternally rolleth the wheel of existence. Everything dieth, everything blossometh forth again; eternally runneth on the year of existence. Everything breaketh, everything is integrated anew; eternally buildeth itself the same house of existence. All things separate, all things again greet one another; eternally true to itself remaineth the ring of existence. *Every moment beginneth existence*; around

every 'Here' rolleth the *ball* 'There.' *The middle is everywhere.* Crooked is the path of eternity.[2]

Nihilism and Regeneration

A second *Leitbild*, arising immediately from the first, is the *Interregnum*: 'We live in an Interregnum: the old order has crumbled; and the new order is not yet visible.' We are on the eve of a 'historical turning' (*Zeitwende*). To the eyes of the men of the *Konservative Revolution*, Nietzsche is the prophet of this 'turning.' Better, he marks this turning in Time when 'something is dead and nothing else is yet born.' One of the most characteristic representatives of the *Konservative Revolution*, the writer Ernst Jünger, also states: 'We are at the turning between two ages, a turning whose meaning is comparable to that of the passage from the Stone Age to the Ages of Metal' (cited by Wulf-Dieter Müller).

In its day-to-day struggle, following the itinerary outlines by Nietzsche, the *Konservative Revolution* adopted the *Leitbild* of nihilism: a positive nihilism whose goal is not nothingness for the sake of nothingness (the end of history, we might say) but the pulverization of the ruins of the old order, the condition *sine qua non* of the new order's advent, of *regeneration* (*Wiedergeburt*). This positive, 'German' or 'Prussian' nihilism advocated by the *Konservative Revolution* is not an end in itself but a means: the means to reach the 'magic point beyond which no man may advance but he who arms himself with new and invisible sources of power' (Ernst Jünger). This 'magic point' is a *Leitbild* in itself: the 'reversal' (*Umschlag*), that is, the *moment* and the *location at which* destruction morphs into creation, *at which* the end reveals itself to be a new beginning. It is the moment *at which* 'each recovers his own origin,' Zarathustra's 'Great Noontide' when historical time is suddenly *regenerated*.

---

2   *Zarathustra*, 'The Convalescent,' 2, tr. Thomas Common; Locchi's emphases. — Tr.

Eternal Returns

All these *Leitbilder* display the preference of the *Konservative Revolution* for formulae that unite antagonistic terms: *Konservative Revolution*, Prussian nihilism, socio-aristocracy, National Bolshevism, etc. True revolution is quite literally '*re*-volution, an about-turn, the reproduction of a moment that has already been.' 'In the beginning was the word,' writes Hans V. Fleig.

> And now present circumstances compel us to pay close attention to the original meaning of the word 'revolution.' During an age of revolution which lasted a hundred and fifty years, Europe has frittered away and left behind the heritage of many centuries. This heritage is the Western community as it was in the spirit of Christianity. Nowadays, foul weather has rusted the Cross and, every way one turns, the Western community disintegrates with startling rapidity. Old gods, whom we thought long murdered by evangelism, go in search of their buried temples. The Western 'superstructure,' this community of Germanic, Latin and Slavic peoples, which traces its roots, in the last analysis, to the Christian *oecumene*, is melting like snow in the sun. in the incandescent fire of a Saturnine star proclaiming the dawn of a new Antiquity, Western thought disintegrates into dust.

Friedrich Hielscher, a disciple of Jünger's, declares: '*Homo revolvens* plays his part on the great world-stage; he will have no peace until the museums have been restocked. The stone altars of sacrifice will stand once more in the clearings; and the crucifixes will be shut up in the museum's cabinets...'

Here, ideology demands an immediate move into political action. But this is always sustained by a *metapolitical vision*. Even Ernst Jünger, a writer inclined to literary botany, cannot suppress this political impulse: his famous *Arbeiter* (*The Worker*) intends to be the manifesto of a 'new politics.' Armin Mohler, sensitive above all to the literary and poetic aspects of the conservative-revolutionary *Weltanschauung*, somewhat neglects those *Leitbilder* more directly bound to political action. Sensing the *historico-temporal* dimensions of the universe he studies with precision and clarity, he is less concerned to discover its *socio-spatial* dimensions.

If Marxism is a theory which must necessarily be prolonged in practice, we might call the *Weltbild* of the *Konservative Revolution* a *metapolitics* that entrusts its ultimate designs on man to *politics*. It therefore seems that, in the eyes of the participants in the *Konservative Revolution*, the 'temporal' *Leitbild* of regeneration has its 'spatial' counterpart in the *Leitbild* of the 'German people' (*Volk*). This is considered the only 'true people,' since it is the *only* people to have preserved the 'conscience of its origins' and, as such, is invested with a 'redemptive' mission from which all mankind will benefit. The *Leitbild* of the "German mission," from Fichte and his famous *Discourse* to Wagner, which Armin Mohler emphasizes somewhat less, is one of the major sources of the *Konservative Revolution*. Similarly, the 'temporal' *Leitbild* of the eternal return and the spherical conception of history corresponds to the 'spatial' *Leitbild* of aristocratic superhumanism and the *hierarchical* conception of society, notions which are also foregrounded in Nietzsche's thinking; and, inversely, the linear conception of history corresponds to the *egalitarian* conception of society.

In the last analysis, the 'conservatives' of the *Konservative Revolution* want to destroy everything that surrounds them: for everything is already a corpse. What they want to *conserve*, we now see clearly, is *man's historicity*—that is, the possibility of *new eternal returns*—as opposed to the 'end of history' offered, explicitly or implicitly, by their adversaries. They work towards the *return of the past*. But this past is not the *past of memory*: it is the *past of an imagination* that plunges its roots into *Sehnsucht*, into a nostalgic and passionate urge towards a regenerated future following the crumbling of civilization.

A Religious Revival

The tendencies that formed within the *Konservative Revolution* might be characterized according to the different *emphases* they placed on different *Leitbilder* belonging to the movement as a whole: images only vaguely discerned by one group played predominant roles in others.

Armin Mohler proposes the classification of these tendencies into five groups: the *Völkischen*, the *Jungkonservativen* ('young' or 'neo-conservatives'), the *Nationalrevolutionäre* ('national revolutionaries'), the *Bündischen* ('leaguists'), and the *Landvolkbewegung* ('peasant movement'). Strictly speaking, these groups were of different natures. The first three, Dr. Mohler specifies, are 'ideological movements' seeing to *realize* their ideas. The other two were 'concrete historical outbursts, from which it was subsequently attempted to draw an ideology.' Nevertheless, it was the former that exercised the greater influence over the political domain.

All three foreground the *Leitbild* of the *Volk*; but each casts a different light on it. For the *Völkischen*, it was a matter of opposing the 'process of disintegration' that endangered the people and of inciting a greater self-consciousness in the people. The *Völkischen* emphasized 'race,' understood as fundamental to the *Volk's* specificity. But their conceptions, even their definitions of *race* were strikingly variable. Some saw it from a purely biological perspective' others saw it as the exemplary unity of 'bodily' and 'spiritual.' While, for Spengler, race is 'that which takes form' (its *own* form), Jünger speaks of 'blood' (*Blut*), but a blood that appears in the 'dazzle' of German Mediaeval mysticism, and still more in the Wagnerian Grail. In fact, there was a profound *völkisch* religiosity which generally sought to express itself in *anti-Christian religious revival*: either the proclamation of a 'German Christianity' or 'German faith' (*Deutschglaube*) or the attempt to resuscitate the cult of ancient deities in a modern context, as with the movement around Ludendorff and his wife Mathilde. The *völkisch* movement also evinced a tendency towards esotericism whose abstruse manifestations sometimes help to discredit the movement. This esotericism permeated, among other the notorious Thule-Gesellschaft to which the poet and dramaturge Dietrich Eckart belonged.

Young Conservatives

On the other hand, the *Jungkonservativen* were primarily concerned to realize the 'mission of the *Volk*,' which was, in their eyes, the construction of a new Empire (*Reich*). Their intellectual leaders, Edgar J. Jung (a future victim of the 'Night of the Long Knives'), Arthur Moeller van den Bruck, Henrich von Gleichen, *etc.*, saw the *Reich* as 'the organization of peoples into a supra-statal whole, dominated by a higher principle, under the supreme responsibility of a single people.' This is not a matter of nationalism, however. The *Jungkonservativen* condemned nationalism, considering it to 'transplant the egotistic doctrines of the individual to the level of the nation-state.' In their vision, the German people is not a people like the rest. It is, as Fichte proclaimed, the only people that has remained 'conscious of its origins' and, consequently, a lone 'true people' in a sea of *mass-peoples*. From this it follows, said Novalis, that 'there are Germans everywhere.' In 1917, a few days before perishing on the Front, the poet Walter Flex, one of the most typical *bündisch* writers, author of the famous song 'Wild Geese' ('*Wildgänse rauschen durch die Nacht*'), wrote:

> If I have spoken of the *eternity of the German people* and the *redemptive mission of Germanness*, it had nothing to do with national egotism. Rather, it was an ethical conviction, perhaps one that realizes itself in defeat or, as Ernst Wurche has written, in the heroic death of a whole people. Nevertheless, I have always imposed a clear limit on this conception. I believe human evolution attaints its most perfect form in the *people* and that universalist humanism implies a *dissolution* inasmuch as it liberates and strips naked the individual egotism till then trammelled by love of one's people...

Meanwhile, Edgar J. Jung declared:

> Peoples are only equal in a metaphysical sense, just as men are only equal before God. He who would transplant this metaphysical equality to the earthly realm sins against nature and against reality. Demographic power, race, intellectual aptitude, historical development, geographical situation:

all this necessitates an earthly hierarchy of peoples, which is not established by chance or by caprice.

In fact, the *Jungkonservativen*, who did not care all that much about philosophy, often thought it possible to reconcile Christian metaphysics with an essentially anti-Christian conception of history. Armin Mohler does not fail to note that this quirk allowed the 'Neo-Conservatives,' alone among the currents of the *Konservative Revolution*, to be admitted as the worthy interlocutor of the Weimar 'system' (and remarks upon the obvious logical contradiction in this peculiarity).

National Bolshevism

Almost to a man, the national revolutionaries were moulded by the experience of the *storms of steel* and 'comradism' of the trenches. For them, the 'nation' is just the *Volk* rallied and 'set in motion' by *war*. The national revolutionaries embraced technological progress not because they succumbed to the 'dangerous temptation to admire it' but because they wanted to 'dominate it — nothing more.' For them, it was a matter, as one of their leaders, Franz Schauwecker, said, of 'doing away with linear time.' Living in the *Interregnum*, they think the time ripe for *positive nihilism*. Their revolutionary urgency and Prussian discipline combine to sustain their will to destroy the 'bourgeois order'; their 'nationalism of soldiers' unites with the 'socialism of comrades.' An acutely *tragic* sense of history and life becomes the backdrop, at once sombre and luminous, of their revolutionary adventure. The deeds of the *Freikorps* ('free corps'), the putsch by the Wikingbund led by Captain Erhardt, the exalted terrorists of the 'outlaws' dramatized by Salomon, the literary attitudes of the 'socio-aristocrat' Jünger, the 'Prussian Socialism' of Oswald Spengler, the Black Front of Otto Strasser, the (old Prussian) dream of an ideological alliance between Bolshevism and the *Konservative Revolution* to bring about a (Germano-Soviet) '*Reich* from Vlissingen to Vladivostok': all this potent but chaotic agitation, thrown together upon the tragedy of a

Germany bruised and humiliated by defeat, lent the emergence of the Weimar Republic its most vivid colours.

Migratory Birds

Contrarily, the *Bund* movement arose before the First World War, growing out of the enormous youth movement (*Jugendbewegund*) in the first years of the century, itself linked to the *Wandervogel* (migratory birds) — a sudden explosion of a particular cast of mind, without definite political persuasion, sweeping across the whole of Germany. With the *Bund*, the youth of the *Interregnum* vaguely discern that the future is at their charge and that the immense task of bringing about the 'return of historical time' falls to them. Above all, the *Bündische Jugend* expresses an attitude to life ruled by a sort of collective unconscious. 'Movement and mobility with no goal,' writes Mohler, 'with no programme, with no ideal but the explosion of the young bourgeois mind into a new *adolescence*, a new, secret, instinctual energy.' At once a 'youth movement' and a 'society of men,' the *Bund* intended to form an elite, bound to disperse, upon coming of age, in all sort of directions, but which was to spread the conservative-revolutionary cast of mind far and wide. In every political camp, left, right and centre, one saw a flourishing of youth-groups (and of paramilitary formations) all nurturing the concerns and preoccupations of the *Konservative Revolution*, sometimes unconsciously and despite declared political persuasions — which explains the surprising developments during the political *Gleichschaltung* (coordination) under the Third Reich.

Armin Mohler saw the *Landvolkbewegung* or 'peasant-movement' as the fifth tendency within the *Konservative Revolution*. In fact, this movement was just a modern *jacquerie*, a spasm of corporative life amidst a teetering and tattered social system. It is nonetheless true that the corporative demands of the *Landvolk*, compelled by circumstance to express themselves politically, fell almost inevitably within the orbit of the *Konservative Revolution*, whose participants heaped it with sincere and vigorous support. It was then undetectably absorbed by National Socialism under the pressure of historical evolution and thanks to the personal efforts of Walther Darré, theoretician of the *Bauernadel* ('peasant aristocracy').

The sentences which end the book have a certain prophetic resonance. 'In the *Konservative Revolution* and its five tendencies,' writes Mohler, 'the ideas of 1789 are confronted with the absolute negation of their values. The struggle which this unleashed is not yet over.' In particular, Armin Mohler believes that today, despite the ideology with which it is linked, this 'confrontation' still carries some germs of the *Konservative Revolution*. Though unaware of it, rendering its agitation vain and sometimes ridiculous, 'the ideas and mythemes of the *Konservative Revolution* are nearly always examined with prejudice, on account of its embarrassing proximity to National Socialism.' 'The situation this creates,' he concludes, 'is nothing new: genuine confrontation of these problems remains the preserve of circles of an esoteric type … while vulgar sects gain strength, whose clumsy and distorting interpretations risk winning over the fanatical masses at any moment.'

Despite its brevity, this final text deserves close attention: for here Locchi not only alludes to the confusion with which his work *America*, or, in the Italian and Spanish translations, *The American Disease*, written collaboratively with Alain de Benoist, was received by some, but also newly advances, in a very condensed form, the idea of a 'projectual' Europe still to be achieved, drawing on Heidegger, which still has the historico-spiritual strength to regenerate its presence in the world and not to die of 'occidentalist alienation.' This text is Giorgio Locchi's response to a question by the journal *Intervento* (no. 69, published under the title 'Europe Is Not an Inheritance: It Is a Future Mission') and later republished in *Margini*, no. 43, a publication of the Edizioni di Ar, July 2003. Its inevitable anachronism (it dates to the time when Europe was still bound by the Treaty of Yalta) removes none of its relevance.

EPILOGUE

Europe Is Not an Inheritance but a Future Mission

THE REAL 'Americanism,' that which threatens our culture, or, more precisely — to put aside this term, 'culture,' which no longer means anything — threatens the soul of Europe, is manifest in the conscious or unconscious adherence to the purported 'American myth' or 'American dream.' This is the 'American disease' from which Europe suffers: a disease which I have attempted to describe in a work written collaboratively with Alain de Benoist.

Europe's 'American' disease, and not America's, as too many readers of this essay have taken it.

A disease, moreover, which does has not come into Europe as an infection but a disease which Europe has always carried internally.

The 'American myth' is none other than the absolutization of 'individualist-liberal-democratic' ideology which, in European societies since the eighteenth century, opposes 'collectivist-socialist-democratic' ideology, which latter is absolutized by the 'Bolshevik myth.' In the aftermath of the War, Europeans certainly wavered between 'American' and 'communist' temptations; but their fate was sealed at Yalta by force of arms compounded by force of geography.

For the last two centuries, European culture has defined itself precisely by this ideological conflict, which is its mortal sickness. In the first half of the twentieth century, the phenomenon called 'fascism' made an attempt to overcome this sickness, an attempt suppressed by the coalition between America and Russia and the ideologies incarnated by America, Russia and the ideological camps gathered round them. The end of the War returned Europe to its internal ideological conflict; but by a decree of history ripened at Yalta, this conflict was now administered and governed on each side of the Iron Curtain by the two superpowers.

Intervento asks whether 'recalling the meaning and identity of Europe outside the logic of two rival blocs is a piety or a viable and realistic solution.' But it is the question itself that is not realistic. The logic of two rival blocs is simply the crudely geopolitical materialization of the logic of rival ideologies of which Europe is the matrix. There no longer exists any European political identity, to the extent that the present situation in Europe stems precisely from the absence of such an identity.

As to the 'meaning' of Europe, this is no doubt found in European civilization or culture: Judaeo-Christian civilization or culture, from which America and Russia directly originate — though each fixes unilaterally on only one fundamental aspect of it. Recalling the meaning and identity of Europe, then, simply means to sink further and further into the shifting sands of the very fate we want to escape. *If we want to talk about Europe, make plans for Europe, we must think of Europe as something which has never been: something whose meaning and identity remain to be invented.* Europe has never been and can never be a 'fatherland,' a 'land of our fathers'; it can never be planned, projected, except, in Nietzsche's words, as a 'land of our sons.'[1]

Escaping the logic of opposite blocs presupposes the renunciation of the very logic of the millennia-old European culture or, more precisely, Western culture: for Europe only exists, is only possible, when it ceases to be the world's West. For as long as Europeans do not renounce this logic, the only effect of any political project will be to nail them to the historic fate determined by Yalta.

---

1   *Thus Spake Zarathustra*, 'Old and New Law-Tables,' 12. — Tr.

In his *Introduction to Metaphysics*, a course given at Freiburg im Breisgau in 1935, but published without corrections in 1953, Martin Heidegger wrote:

> This Europe, in its unholy blindness always on the point cutting its own throat, lies today in the great pincers between Russia on the one side and America on the other. Russia and America, seen metaphysically, are both the same. [...] We lie in the pincers. [...I]f the great decision regarding Europe is not to go down the path of annihilation — precisely then can this decision come about only through the development of *historically new* spiritual forces. [... T]his means nothing less than to repeat and retrieve [*wieder-holen*] the inception of our historical-spiritual existence [*Anfang unseres geschichtlich-geistigen Daseins*], in order to transform it into a *new* inception. Such a thing is possible. [...] But an inception is not repeated when one shrinks back to it as something that once was, something that by now is familiar and is simply to be imitated, but rather when the inception is begun again *more originally*, and with all the strangeness, darkness, insecurity that a genuine inception brings with it.[2]

---

2   Martin Heidegger, *Introduction to Metaphysics*, tr. Gregory Fried and Richard Polt (New Haven: Yale University Press, 2000), pp. 40–1. Amended to follow Locchi's version. — Tr.

L'Institut Iliade for Long European Memory

L'Institut Iliade for Long European Memory, based in France, was born from an observation. Europe is but a shadow of her former self. Replaced by outsiders, confused by having lost their bearing and their pride, Europeans have abandoned the reins of their common destiny to people other than themselves. Europeans no longer remember. Why? Because amongst the current elite — whether at school, university, or in the media — no one passes down to them the cultural wealth of which they are the inheritors.

Contrary to this moribund current, L'Institut Iliade has given itself the task of participating in the renewal of the cultural grandeur of Europe and in aiding Europeans' reappropriation of their own identity. Facing the Great Erasure of culture, we intend to work for the Great Awakening of European consciousness and to help prepare Europe for a new renaissance — one of identity, freedom, and power.

L'Institut Iliade's calling is threefold:

- To train young men and young women concerned about their history to always build. To make them the avantgarde of the renaissance for which the Institut calls: men and women capable of giving to civic and political action that cultural and metapolitical dimension which is indispensable. Their motto: to put themselves at the service of a community of destiny, which risks disappearing if it is not taken in hand. Armed with a strong culture relating to European traditions and values, they learn to discern that the adventure that awaits them entails risks and self-sacrifice, but also enthusiasm and joy.

- To promote a radical and alternative vision of the world contrary to the dogmas of universalism, egalitarianism, and 'diversity'. Using all available means, the Institut develops concepts and ammunition to understand and fight the modern world.
- To gather together, especially — but not only — in France, those who refuse to submit and who are inspired daily by the Homeric triad as described by Dominique Venner: nature as the base, excellence as the goal, beauty as the horizon.

L'Institut Iliade's originality, especially with the aim of reformulating and updating knowledge, lies in tying together the seriousness of its content with ease of learning for the greater public, the objective being to demonstrate an authentic pedagogy, and to act in complementary or supportive ways with other initiatives having the same goal.

L'Institut Iliade's action takes place across various channels:

- A cadre school of the European Rebirth, which every year brings together trainees from a wide variety of backgrounds and is already seeing citizens from other European countries participate;
- an annual colloquium — made up of academics, politicians, writers, journalists, and association officials from all over Europe — that meets in Paris to discuss strong and challenging themes, such as 'The Aesthetic Universe of Europeans', 'Facing the Migratory Assault', 'Transmit or Disappear', 'Nature as Base — for an Ecology of Place', 'Beyond the Market — Economy at the Service of Peoples';
- the publication of works — designed as beacons to enlighten readers' thoughts and guide them toward the reconquest of their

identity — within several collections, made available in the widest array of languages and European countries;
- artistic exhibitions on the fringes of contemporary artistic trends, allowing the public to take a fresh look at art and rooted creation;
- an incubator for ideas, businesses, and associations to support and help the greatest number of projects — with quality and sustainability criteria — across all fields of civil society (culture, commerce, etc.) that seek to impose a rooted vision of the world and an alternative to the current system, while prioritising structures and projects making an impact in real life;
- an active presence on social media, allowing us to reach new audiences (through videos, publications, annual events, and news presentations), centred around a website that functions as much as a resource hub as it does as a platform for exchanges and debate, notably offering an ideal library of more than five hundred works, a European primer, a dictionary of quotations, and turnkey itineraries for visiting and hiking the prominent places of European memory.

Education through history:

L'Institut Iliade endeavours to uphold in every circumstance the richness and singularity of our heritage in order to draw forth the source and the resources of a serene, but determined, affirmation of our identity, both national and European. In line with the thought and deeds of Dominique Venner, the Institut accords in all its activities an essential place to history, both as a matrix of deep meditation on the future as well as a place of the unexpected, where anything is possible.

Concerning Europe, it seems as though we will be forced to rise up and face immense challenges and fearsome catastrophes even beyond those posed by immigration. These hardships will present the opportunity for both a rebirth and a rediscovery of ourselves. I believe in those qualities that are specific to the European people, qualities currently in a state of dormancy. I believe in our active individuality, our inventiveness, and in the awakening of our energy. This awakening will undoubtedly come. When? I do not know, but I am positive that it will take place.

— Dominique Venner, *The Shock of History*
Arktos Media, London, 2015

Follow L'Institut Iliade at
www.institut-iliade.com
linktr.ee/InstitutILIADE

OTHER BOOKS PUBLISHED BY ARKTOS

Virginia Abernethy	Born Abroad
Sri Dharma Pravartaka Acharya	The Dharma Manifesto
Joakim Andersen	Rising from the Ruins
Winston C. Banks	Excessive Immigration
Stephen Baskerville	Who Lost America?
Alain de Benoist	Beyond Human Rights
	Carl Schmitt Today
	The Ideology of Sameness
	The Indo-Europeans
	Manifesto for a European Renaissance
	On the Brink of the Abyss
	The Problem of Democracy
	Runes and the Origins of Writing
	View from the Right (vol. 1–3)
Armand Berger	Tolkien, Europe, and Tradition
Arthur Moeller van den Bruck	Germany's Third Empire
Matt Battaglioli	The Consequences of Equality
Kerry Bolton	The Perversion of Normality
	Revolution from Above
	Yockey: A Fascist Odyssey
Isac Boman	Money Power
Charles William Dailey	The Serpent Symbol in Tradition
Ricardo Duchesne	Faustian Man in a Multicultural Age
Alexander Dugin	Ethnos and Society
	Ethnosociology
	Eurasian Mission
	The Fourth Political Theory
	The Great Awakening vs the Great Reset
	Last War of the World-Island
	Politica Aeterna
	Political Platonism
	Putin vs Putin
	The Rise of the Fourth Political Theory
	Templars of the Proletariat
	The Theory of a Multipolar World
Edward Dutton	Race Differences in Ethnocentrism
Mark Dyal	Hated and Proud
Clare Ellis	The Blackening of Europe
Koenraad Elst	Return of the Swastika
Julius Evola	The Bow and the Club
	Fascism Viewed from the Right
	A Handbook for Right-Wing Youth
	Metaphysics of Power
	Metaphysics of War
	The Myth of the Blood
	Notes on the Third Reich
	Pagan Imperialism

OTHER BOOKS PUBLISHED BY ARKTOS

	Recognitions
	A Traditionalist Confronts Fascism
Guillaume Faye	*Archeofuturism*
	Archeofuturism 2.0
	The Colonisation of Europe
	Convergence of Catastrophes
	Ethnic Apocalypse
	A Global Coup
	Prelude to War
	Sex and Deviance
	Understanding Islam
	Why We Fight
Daniel S. Forrest	*Suprahumanism*
Andrew Fraser	*Dissident Dispatches*
	Reinventing Aristocracy in the Age of Woke Capital
	The WASP Question
Génération Identitaire	*We are Generation Identity*
Peter Goodchild	*The Taxi Driver from Baghdad*
	The Western Path
Paul Gottfried	*War and Democracy*
Petr Hampl	*Breached Enclosure*
Porus Homi Havewala	*The Saga of the Aryan Race*
Lars Holger Holm	*Hiding in Broad Daylight*
	Homo Maximus
	Incidents of Travel in Latin America
	The Owls of Afrasiab
Richard Houck	*Liberalism Unmasked*
A. J. Illingworth	*Political Justice*
Institut Iliade	*For a European Awakening*
	Guardians of Heritage
Alexander Jacob	*De Naturae Natura*
Jason Reza Jorjani	*Artemis Unveiled*
	Closer Encounters
	Erosophia
	Faustian Futurist
	Iranian Leviathan
	Lovers of Sophia
	Novel Folklore
	Philosophy of the Future
	Prometheism
	Promethean Pirate
	Prometheus and Atlas
	Psychotron
	Uber Man
	World State of Emergency
Henrik Jonasson	*Sigmund*

OTHER BOOKS PUBLISHED BY ARKTOS

Edgar Julius Jung	*The Significance of the German Revolution*
Ruuben Kaalep & August Meister	*Rebirth of Europe*
Roderick Kaine	*Smart and SeXy*
Peter King	*Here and Now*
	Keeping Things Close
	On Modern Manners
James Kirkpatrick	*Conservatism Inc.*
Ludwig Klages	*The Biocentric Worldview*
	Cosmogonic Reflections
	The Science of Character
Andrew Korybko	*Hybrid Wars*
Pierre Krebs	*Guillaume Faye: Truths & Tributes*
	Fighting for the Essence
Julien Langella	*Catholic and Identitarian*
John Bruce Leonard	*The New Prometheans*
Stephen Pax Leonard	*The Ideology of Failure*
	Travels in Cultural Nihilism
William S. Lind	*Reforging Excalibur*
	Retroculture
Pentti Linkola	*Can Life Prevail?*
H. P. Lovecraft	*The Conservative*
Norman Lowell	*Imperium Europa*
Richard Lynn	*Sex Differences in Intelligence*
	A Tribute to Helmut Nyborg (ed.)
John MacLugash	*The Return of the Solar King*
Charles Maurras	*The Future of the Intelligentsia &*
	For a French Awakening
John Harmon McElroy	*Agitprop in America*
Michael O'Meara	*Guillaume Faye and the Battle of Europe*
	New Culture, New Right
Michael Millerman	*Beginning with Heidegger*
Dmitry Moiseev	*The Philosophy of Italian Fascism*
Maurice Muret	*The Greatness of Elites*
Brian Anse Patrick	*The NRA and the Media*
	Rise of the Anti-Media
	The Ten Commandments of Propaganda
	Zombology
Tito Perdue	*The Bent Pyramid*
	Journey to a Location
	Lee
	Morning Crafts
	Philip
	The Sweet-Scented Manuscript
	William's House (vol. 1–4)
John K. Press	*The True West vs the Zombie Apocalypse*
Raido	*A Handbook of Traditional Living* (vol. 1–2)

OTHER BOOKS PUBLISHED BY ARKTOS

P R Reddall	*Towards Awakening*
Claire Rae Randall	*The War on Gender*
Steven J. Rosen	*The Agni and the Ecstasy*
	The Jedi in the Lotus
Nicholas Rooney	*Talking to the Wolf*
Richard Rudgley	*Barbarians*
	Essential Substances
	Wildest Dreams
Ernst von Salomon	*It Cannot Be Stormed*
	The Outlaws
Werner Sombart	*Traders and Heroes*
Piero San Giorgio	*Giuseppe*
	Survive the Economic Collapse
	Surviving the Next Catastrophe
Sri Sri Ravi Shankar	*Celebrating Silence*
	Know Your Child
	Management Mantras
	Patanjali Yoga Sutras
	Secrets of Relationships
George T. Shaw (ed.)	*A Fair Hearing*
Fenek Solère	*Kraal*
	Reconquista
Oswald Spengler	*The Decline of the West*
	Man and Technics
Richard Storey	*The Uniqueness of Western Law*
Tomislav Sunic	*Against Democracy and Equality*
	Homo Americanus
	Postmortem Report
	Titans are in Town
Askr Svarte	*Gods in the Abyss*
Hans-Jürgen Syberberg	*On the Fortunes and Misfortunes of Art in Post-War Germany*
Abir Taha	*Defining Terrorism*
	The Epic of Arya (2nd ed.)
	Nietzsche is Coming God, or the Redemption of the Divine
	Verses of Light
Jean Thiriart	*Europe: An Empire of 400 Million*
Bal Gangadhar Tilak	*The Arctic Home in the Vedas*
Dominique Venner	*For a Positive Critique*
	The Shock of History
Hans Vogel	*How Europe Became American*
Markus Willinger	*A Europe of Nations*
	Generation Identity
Alexander Wolfheze	*Alba Rosa*
	Globus Horribilis
	Rupes Nigra

www.ingramcontent.com/pod-product-compliance
Lightning Source LLC
Chambersburg PA
CBHW032226080426
42735CB00008B/725